FEB 2 1 2012

D1212480

Chess for the Gifted and Busy

A short but comprehensive course— from beginner to expert

by GM Lev Alburt and Al Lawrence

Poor Condition_____
Marks/Stains X_____
GVK Date 11/22/17 LE

GLENVIEW PUBLIC LIBRARY
1930 Glenview Road
Glenview, IL 60025

Published by:
Chess Information and Research Center
P.O. Box 534, Gracie Station, New York, New York 10028
Telephone: 212.794.8706
and
OutExcel! Corp.
289 Borden Road, Wallkill, New York 12589
Email: al@outexcel.com

For ordering information
Please see page 304.

Distribution to the book trade by:
W.W. Norton, 500 Fifth Avenue, New York, New York

Editing & Design
OutExcel! Corporation
Email: al@outexcel.com
Cover Design Jami L. Anson

© Copyright 2012 (first edition) by Lev Alburt and Al Lawrence.
All rights reserved.

ISBN: 978-1-889323-24-4
Library of Congress Catalog Card Number: 2011940902

10 9 8 7 6 5 4 3 2 1

Printed in the United States of America.

"You sit at the board and suddenly your heart leaps. Your hand trembles to pick up the piece and move it. But what chess teaches you is that you must sit there calmly and think about whether it's really a good idea and whether there are other, better ideas."

—Stanley Kubrick

Important Note to the Reader

This book began some years ago as a brash "thought experiment." Could the two of us really construct a course that would perhaps take years off the quest for chess expertise, even for a complete beginner? We thought it possible.

One of us, Grandmaster Lev Alburt, a three-time U.S. Chess Champion, three-time Ukrainian Champion and former European Champion, is a world-famous and sought-after chess teacher. The other, Al Lawrence, is the winner of many national awards for writing about chess, as well as being the former executive director of the U.S. Chess Federation and later director of the World Chess Hall of Fame. Al is also a former high school and university teacher, with advanced degrees in education. We'd worked together for fifteen years to complete the *Comprehensive Chess Course*, a bookshelf of 14 volumes that can take a reader from beginner to master. Could we carefully construct a single, condensed book that would give a bright and busy reader the core curriculum? It was an exciting challenge.

Chess for the Gifted and Busy is, we feel, the very successful result. In one book of about 300 pages, you get all the information required to be a very strong player—plus some guidance to continue, if you choose, on a quest for outright chess mastery.

Whether you want to learn chess yourself or teach it to your child, there are obviously lots of other activities you also have on your agenda. This book provides you the fastest way to learn to play chess. At the same time, it comprehensively supplies you the important winning knowledge of both strategy and tactics. What's left out?—for one thing, the amount of repetition generally demanded by other instructional books. This book requires your attention and a reasonable amount of dedication, particularly to the exercises we include. Another time-saver is turning "baby-steps" into reasonable strides of learning. If you're a beginner, this special curriculum requires that you study the chapters in order, because the program is carefully constructed in a "spiraling staircase" of information and skill-building.

Perhaps best of all, you select your goal from one of three possible levels. If you want to go from absolute beginner to neighborhood champ, you can literally complete Level I in a single afternoon, play some practice games—and be confounding the block champ before you know it! When you're ready to become a tough tournament-level competitor, Level II cuts through the mysteries of strategy and tactics to show you precisely what you need to know. And, if you decide that you won't settle for anything less than being an Expert, near the top levels of tournament chess, Level III puts you on the path to being a tournament champion!

If you are already a chess player, *Chess for the Gifted and Busy* will fill in the gaps preventing you from chess excellence. And it provides the most time-efficient review of important techniques for chess veterans, even master-level players.

A few words on how to best use the book

Obviously, studying examples is an important way that we learn. And when we examine a chess game, we look at what was or should be played, and often what wasn't or shouldn't be played. To make all this easy to follow, we give "main line" variations (what was or should be played) in bold print and in larger diagrams. (Diagrams are "snapshots" of the position of pieces on the chessboard.) We give the "sidelines" in regular print and smaller diagrams. Once you start reading, you'll see that this makes following along much easier.

You will be able to read much of this book without a board and set, but we recommend that you do have your own chessmen on your own board while going through the variations. The diagrams we provide will help you to check to make sure you have the right positions as you go along.

We emphasize many important rules and guiding principles in larger type. Importantly, at the end of most chapters, we provide you "puzzles," in the form of chess diagrams, to solve. Work at solving these before going to the solutions. Doing so will not only help to lock what you've learned into your memory, but will in many cases expand on what you've learned—in other words these "Memory Markers" are "enrichment" and "discovery" material. And when you do play over the solutions, make sure you understand the ideas thoroughly before moving on.

In this book we cite the wisdom of some of the game's greatest players from a number of centuries. We also sometimes make use of the most modern chess resource, the powerful new chess "engines"—chess programs that see dozens of moves ahead with absolute clarity and provide evaluations of the most complex positions. They are not infallible, since they do lack human intuition, but are the next best thing. We used two programs recognized as the best at the time of this writing—Rybka and Houdini. As time goes on, we will add exercises and tips online at www.chesswithlev.com, and we hope you'll join us there.

Chess for the Gifted and Busy is a condensed but comprehensive summary of the entire *Comprehensive Chess Course* series, also available from W.W. Norton.

Enjoy your journey of discovery and personal growth into the world's greatest strategy game! You can email us your comments at al@outexcel.com.

—Grandmaster Lev Alburt and Al Lawrence, New York, October 25, 2011

Table of Contents
Chess for the Gifted and Busy

Books by Lev Alburt
and Al Lawrence

Chess Rules of Thumb
Three Days with Bobby Fischer
Chess Training Pocket Book II
Chess for the Gifted and Busy

More Books by Lev Alburt

Comprehensive Chess Course, Volume 1
Comprehensive Chess Course, Volume 2
Chess Tactics for the Tournament Player
The King in Jeopardy
Chess Strategy
Chess Training Pocket Book
Just the Facts!
Pirc Alert!
Building Up Your Chess
Chess Openings for White, Explained
Chess Openings for Black, Explained

Lev Alburt's co-authors include Roman Pelts, Sam Palatnik,
Nikolay Krogius, Alex Chernin, Roman Dzindzichashvili, and Eugene Perelshteyn.

To order, please see page 304.

The Benefits of Chess

Since the 1970s, serious studies have touted and documented the many benefits of chess. Chess improves a host of important skills. among them: concentration, logical and critical thinking, memory, patience, persistence, self-confidence, self-control, sportsmanship, and respect for others. Parents and teachers have seen these benefits first-hand as they see record numbers of youngsters competing in scholastic chess programs.

But the mental and emotional benefits of chess apply to all ages. Even some pre-school children have learned and benefited from chess, and so have senior citizens. Most of us learn somewhere in between these two landmarks. But it is never too late to learn.

Perhaps most of all, chess reminds us of the thrill of authentic mental challenge and of cerebral competition. The authors feel chess is the most beneficial one-on-one thinking game in the world. Wherever you go in the world, you will find others who enjoy the challenge of the Royal Game.

If you're like us, you have a lot more fun when you're pretty good at something. But we all have many demands on our time—whether obligations like school and work or recreational activities we enjoy. Being good at chess should not have to be an all-or-nothing choice! That's why we've written this book—to provide a way that you can become truly good at chess in a short period of time.

**"A few strong instincts
and a few plain rules
will suffice us."**

—Ralph Waldo Emerson

—Level I—

Lesson One

The Rules of Play

By the end of this lesson, you'll know all the legal moves.
You'll be able to play a real game of chess with anyone.

First things first, you need to know about the board we play on and how the chessmen move. Keep in mind that there are no "house rules" about how the chessmen move. The moves are the same all over the world.

The goal

Even if you don't know the first thing about the board or the chessmen, let's begin by making the object of a chess game clear: You want to win by *checkmating* your opponent's king—placing his king under attack in a way that it cannot escape. That's it. The goal is simple.

The board

Although most people concentrate exclusively on the capabilities of the chessmen when learning the game, it is equally important to know the "field" the men play on. Don't skip learning the board well in your impatience to get to the moves of the men and other rules! You should reach the point that you can visualize the files and diagonals of the board and the colors of the individual squares. As always, we'll take you through the important points as speedily as possible— you'll be playing soon enough.

The chessboard is a square made up of 64 smaller squares. The colors of the squares alternate between dark and light. The board is made up of:

• Eight horizontal rows, called *ranks*

• Eight vertical rows, called *files*

• Light and dark *diagonals*— diagonals crisscross the whole board and vary in length from two to eight squares.

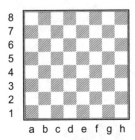

Chess can be played on any 8-square x 8-square board, as long as the chessmen you're using don't seem crowded on it. In a pinch, you can even use those folding, red-and-black boards found in inexpensive checker sets.

Whatever board you use, when you set up for a game, *always* make sure that a light square is at the far right from each player's perspective.

Some chessboards will have borders numbering the ranks from 1-8 and giving letters to the files from a-h. (We've shown such a border in the diagram above to make this clear. And we'll repeat this border, to help you get started, on the smaller diagrams throughout this first lesson.) A bit later, we'll explain why. For now, note that such boards can be helpful when you are learning, but aren't necessary. Tournament players use boards with or without these borders. Both are "legal" equipment.

The chessmen

Chess is a two-player game and begins with two equal armies, one light-colored and one darker—referred to as "white" and "black" regardless of their actual colors. Each chess army is made of 16 chessmen. There are eight *pieces* and eight *pawns* in each army. (Pawns are not called "pieces"; they are too lowly to be awarded this status.)

How the chessmen move

Each kind of chessman moves differently. Although there are 16 chessmen in each army, there are duplicates, so there are really only six different types of chessmen and their different movements to learn. It will take only a few pages for you to learn how the pieces move. Along the way you'll see where every piece stands at the begin-

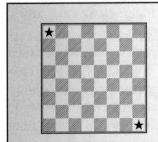

**Remember—
Light
on
Right!**

ning of a game—each game of chess starts from the same startup position.

First, some general rules about moving the pieces:

1. White always moves first, and the players take turns making one move at a time.

2. Chess pieces are never forced to capture (chess is not checkers!), unless a capture is the only legal move available.

3. Only one piece at a time can occupy a square.

4. When you capture an enemy piece or pawn (you can't capture your own men), you remove the enemy man from its square, take it off the board and replace it with your piece or pawn to complete your move.

The rook

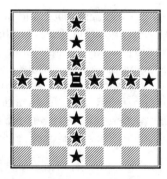

We begin with the rook because its move is intuitive. At the beginning of the game, each side has two rooks. Think of the rook as a sort of SUV and think of the ranks and files as roads.

The rook-SUV can go straight ahead and in reverse, or it can turn left or right. On an empty board, a rook can move in a straight line in one direction as many squares as the player moving it desires. The stars in the diagram at the bottom of the left-hand column mark the 14 squares available to a rook on an otherwise empty board.

Rooks are one of the two types of major pieces. A major piece, with the help of its king, can force a lone enemy king into checkmate. More on this later.

Setting up the chessmen:

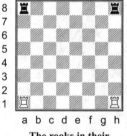

**The rooks in their
starting positions**

White moves up

Chess diagrams (representations of the chessboard and pieces in print, like the one above) normally show white starting from the "bottom" and moving his pawns "up" the board. This tradition allows chess players to quickly orient themselves in any published position, without even knowing how the game began. Without this publishing convention, it might not otherwise be clear which way the pawns are moving! (As you'll soon see, pawns move only foreward.)

One more thing—to keep the explanations simple, in this first lesson we use some diagrams that don't really show you a legal chess position. (For example, there could never be an actual game position without a white and a black king on the board.) After Lesson I, all the diagrams will represent legal positions that could occur in real chess games.

The king

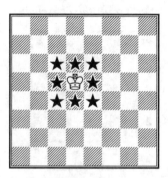

Each army has only one king, of course. The king's move is another one simple to learn. On the empty board above, he can move to any square he is next

to. The stars mark the eight squares that the king can move to in this position. Suppose the board is not empty. Then, like all the other pieces, the king cannot move to a square occupied by another member of his own army.

The king is unique because it cannot be captured. That's why any legal chess position must contain both a white and a black king. (Remember, checkmate ends the game.)

There is another important caveat—the king cannot move to a square *attacked* by an enemy man. (He would be moving into *check*, as explained below.)

Thus, the two opposing kings can never stand on squares next to each other, because one would have had to move into check, exposing itself to capture.

Let's look at what could be a real game position. (See the diagram in the left-hand column of the facing page.) The white king is on the same square as in the diagram at left. But we've added some pieces. Squares available to the white king are once again

Checkmate
—the imminent and unavoidable capture of the king—
ends the game.

Real kings never kiss!
The kings can never stand
on squares next to each other.

marked with stars. On the other hand, Xs mark the squares the king *could* move to—except for the fact they are attacked by enemy pieces.

The white king above has only three available moves. The white king's mobility is cut off by the black rook that controls the whole rank in front of the monarch. Another square, immediately behind the white king, is occupied by his own rook. A final taboo square, behind and to the right of the white king, is off limits because the black king controls that square.

In addition to the moves we've just learned, the king and rook are involved in *castling*, one of the four special moves we discuss at the end of this lesson.

Setting up the chessmen:

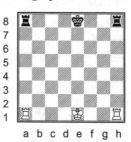

The rooks and kings in their starting positions

Check always takes precedence

Only a king can be placed *in check*. A king is said to be in check when he stands on a square attacked by an enemy piece. Since a king can never be captured, his highness must get out of check immediately—his army can't do anything else until its king is out of check. He has three ways to do this.

1. The checked king can move out of check;

2. The checking piece can be captured;

3. A friendly piece can block the check—stepping in between the enemy attacker and the king.

We'll see examples of all these later in the book. But for now it's important to know that if a checked king doesn't have any of these three defenses available to it, it's check*mate*, and his side loses immediately!

And as we've just seen, a king may never move into check.

Checkmate ends the game

Now that you know how the rooks and king move, we can show you an example of every chess player's goal—checkmate.

Take a look at the position below.

White has checkmated black using the king and rook.

The white rook attacks the enemy king—putting it in check. At the same time, the white king barricades the escape squares on the seventh rank. The black king cannot escape check—and that's called check*mate*. (This word comes from two Persian words—*shah*, meaning king; and *mat*, meaning dead: "king dead." Keep that in mind and you won't forget the ultimate goal of chess!)

Black uses his rook to checkmate white's king.

White is attacked by the black rook and can't escape, embarrassingly enough, because the king's own retinue of attendant pawns hem him in. (Pawns can't move backward to block the check.) His entourage is protecting him from a frontal attack but has been outflanked by the rook. This type of checkmate is actually so common that it has a name—*back-rank mate*.

The queen

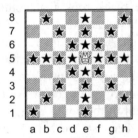

Each army has only one queen, and her move is like the king's—she can move in any

Checkmate ends the game.

When setting up the pieces, remember: "Queens love their own color!"
White queen on a light square;
Black queen on a dark square.

direction, along the ranks and files, plus the diagonals. But she can move an *unlimited* number of squares in any direction until she decides to stop or runs into another chessman! In the center of the empty board, she shows you why she is the most powerful piece. She can move to any of the 27 starred squares, more than 40% of the board!

The queen is the other *major* piece. With her king's help, she can force checkmate against a lone enemy king.

Because the queen is so powerful, checkmating with your queen and king is even easier than checkmating with your rook and king.

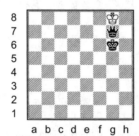

Black has used his king and queen
to checkmate white's king.

In the preceding diagram, with white's king against the edge of the board, black's queen both attacks white's king (thus putting him in check) and covers all the enemy monarch's possible escape squares. Black's queen is supported by her king. Because the white king may not move into check to capture her, and since he cannot avoid capture, he is in checkmate. The game is over. Black wins.

Setting up the chessmen:

**The rooks, kings, and queens
in their starting positions**

Notice that the white queen is always set up to begin the game on a light square and that the black queen always starts on a dark square. "The queen loves her own color."

Your two bishops travel in parallel universes!

The bishop

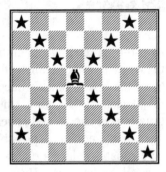

Each army has two bishops, which move only along the diagonals. Like the queens and rooks, bishops can move an unlimited number of squares in any direction until they decide to stop or run into another piece. In the center of the empty board above, the bishop can move to 13 different squares.

The bishop is one of the two *minor* pieces. Even with the help of its own king, a single bishop cannot force checkmate against a lone enemy king.

Your two bishops never touch

A bishop begins the game on one color square and *never leaves that color*! One of your bishops begins on a dark square and must stay only on the dark squares. The other begins on the light squares and must never stray from them. Each of your bishops (and your opponent's) can travel on only 32 of the 64 squares of the chessboard.

Enemy bishops on different color squares are called "bishops of opposite color." They can never land on or control the same squares.

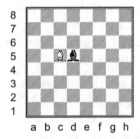

These enemy bishops can never capture each other. They can never threaten the same square.

Setting up the chessmen:

The rooks, kings, queens and bishops in their starting positions

The knight

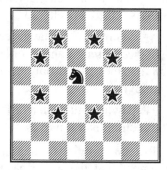

Each army has two knights. Their unusual and tricky method of moving adds magic to the chessboard.

The knight can travel in any direction and its move has been explained in various ways. The most common advice is to see its move as an "L." You can think of its move as a combination of moves: one square horizontally and two moves vertically—or two squares horizontally and one vertically. Chess expert Jack Winters, always a contrarian, used to insist that the knight moves one square as a rook and then one as a bishop, but this comes to the same thing, of course. So use whatever description helps you the most. With a bit of practice, you'll know the knight's move without thinking.

The knight is the other *minor* piece. Even with the help of its own king, it cannot force checkmate against a lone enemy king.

Recall how the bishops are each limited to the color squares they start the game on? Well, the knight can get to all squares of the board—but on each of his moves, the color the knight lands on *alternates*. If the knight stands on a light square, then its only moves are to black squares, and then its next move is to a light square again. In the previous diagram, we saw the knight on a light square. Let's look at its possible moves from a dark square.

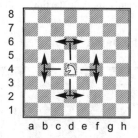

The knight's move is L-shaped and it must land on alternate-color squares. From this dark square, it can go to eight light squares.

Special equestrian powers

The knight has an ability unique among the chessmen. A knight can *jump*! (Of course, it's a horse!) Even the powerful queen must keep her regal feet on the board. Since the knight can hop over other pieces and pawns, whether they're friend or foe, a

The knight has the unique power to leap!

knight's threat can never be blocked. That means the knight can sometimes be particularly effective in blocked positions.

Setting up the chessmen:

The rooks, kings, queens, bishops and knights in their starting positions

The pawn

Our final chessman to learn is the pawn. The pawn is technically not a piece. It lacks the rank of the nobler chessmen we've looked at. It is the foot soldier of chess. Like the lowest-ranking members of any army, pawns stand in front, and are often true cannon fodder.

A pawn has some unique qualities:

• A pawn can move only *straight ahead, one square* at a time. (Retreat or fancy maneuvering is left to its betters.)

• Exception: A pawn can move *two squares* ahead on its very first move (and only on its first move).

• A pawn captures in a different direction than it moves.

In the previous diagram, remember that the white pawns can move only "up" the board. Notice that the pawn on the right, in its original position, has the *option* to move one or two squares ahead. But its comrade on the left has already moved from his original square. So that pawn has no two-square option.

Pawns capture diagonally

Think of the pawn as an ancient Roman foot soldier holding a shield in front of him with one hand and a short sword in his other hand. To use his sword, he must poke it diagonally, to the side of his shield. That's how a pawn captures. Study the diagram below to decide what possible pawn moves white has.

**White to move:
What are all the possible pawn moves?**

In the previous diagram, the white pawn on the left has no moves. Its straight-ahead progress is barricaded by the enemy pawn.

The white pawn on the right, however, has three possible moves:

1. It can move straight ahead one square.

2. It can capture the black bishop, diagonally to the right.

3. It can capture the black pawn, diagonally to the left.

Additionally, the pawn can make two truly special moves we discuss at the end of this lesson.

The complete chess armies, ready to start a game:

All of the chess pieces and pawns in their starting positions

Four Special Moves

There are only four moves left to learn before you know everything about how the pieces move: castling, pawn promotion, *en passant*, and stalemate.

Castling

Castling is the only chess move that permits a player to move two of his pieces at once. Castling is a key move because it gets your king out of the center, where it is most vulnerable, and gets your rook out of the corner and into the game, where it can better exercise its considerable powers. Because of these dual benefits, castling is seen in almost every master game.

To castle, the king moves two squares to the left or right from its original square toward one of his rooks. The rook lands on the square on the other side of the king.

When a player castles toward the rook he's closest to, it's called *castling kingside* or *castling short*.

Both the white and black kings have castled kingside (short).

When a player castles toward the farther-away rook, on the other side of his queen, it's called *castling queenside* or *castling long*.

Both the white and black kings have castled queenside (long).

In order to castle, these four conditions must be met:

1. Neither the rook involved nor the king may have moved previously. (Thus each side can castle only once during the game.)

2. No chessman of either color can stand between the rook involved and the king.

3. The king can't castle out of check.

4. While castling, the king cannot pass over a square controlled by the enemy.

Pawn promotion

If a pawn can make it to the other side of the board, it can be promoted to any chess piece other than a king. (In this way, even when the armies have dwindled down to opposing kings and a pawn or two, the threat of checkmate after a promotion still makes for exciting chess.)

A pawn is normally promoted to a queen because she is the most powerful piece. Through promotion, there can be several queens of the same color on the board. (One is usually enough!) But, theoretically, through promotion, there could be many bishops, knights or rooks on the board.

En passant

This French phrase, meaning "in passing" has stuck as the name for a tricky pawn option that was invented to keep a pawn from avoiding capture by using its opportunity on its first move to advance two squares. Here's the easiest way to understand *en passant*:

If a pawn advances two squares on its first move, and there is an enemy pawn that *could have captured it if it had moved only one square*—then the enemy pawn has the option of doing just that. Let's take a look:

White's pawn can advance to the starred square but is still vulnerable to capture as if it had moved only one square!

If the white pawn advances one square, it could be captured by the black pawn. If the white pawn uses its option to advance two squares, the black pawn can capture it with exactly the same result. (You can think of it as pushing the pawn back one square and then capturing it.) In both cases, the resulting board would look like this:

After the *en passant* move, above.

Stalemate

Our last special move is stalemate. Strictly speaking, stalemate isn't so much a type of move as it is a special condition. Stalemate occurs when one side is on move but has no legal moves, and his king is *not* in check. (This last fact is the key and only difference between stalemate and checkmate.)

Stalemate is a draw, so it's a very different result than checkmate! Here are a few stalemate positions:

Black, on move, has no legal options. Since he's not in check, it's stalemate.

It's white's move. It's stalemate: he can't move and he's not in check.

At the end of most chapters, we give you "puzzle" positions ("Memory Markers") to think about and solve.
Try to find the best move before looking at the solutions.
It may help to set up the position on your own board and play over different tries, or "variations."

Stalemate ends the game in a draw!

Special Tip for the Gifted and Busy

The Value of the Chessmen

In every chess game you play, it's highly likely you'll trade your pieces for your opponent's.

But all chessmen were not created equal. Some (the pawns) are infantry "grunts," while others (rooks, for example) are more like long-range artillery. And of course, there's the king, who can't be traded. You have to know which men are worth more than others to avoid getting shortchanged when exchanging. So let's look at the relative value of the different kinds of chessmen.

♛ = 9 points

♜ = 5 points

♝ = 3 points

♞ = 3 points

♟ = 1 point

Level I, Lesson One
Memory Markers!

Black to move   **Black to move**

After 1. ... b7-b5+   **White to move**

Solutions:

MM1: 1. ... Nf7#.

MM2: 1. ... f1=N+, winning material—after 2. K-(any), Nxd2.

MM3: 1. axb6+ ep (White's only move. The game is even.)

MM4: 1. Be3, winning black's pawn on a7. Note that 1. Bb8 allows
        1. ... Bd4, defending the pawn.

Chess Notation

Chess players around the world use "notation," a universal system for reading and writing chess. It's easy to learn, and once you know it, you'll be able to decipher quickly any book or newspaper article on chess.

The vertical columns of squares that run up and down the board are called *files* and are lettered. The horizontal rows of squares that run sideways are called *ranks* and are numbered. The intersection of a *file* and *rank* gives a square its name. Let's look at a board that gives the "address" of every square:

a8	b8	c8	d8	e8	f8	g8	h8
a7	b7	c7	d7	e7	f7	g7	h7
a6	b6	c6	d6	e6	f6	g6	h6
a5	b5	c5	d5	e5	f5	g5	h5
a4	b4	c4	d4	e4	f4	g4	h4
a3	b3	c3	d3	e3	f3	g3	h3
a2	b2	c2	d2	e2	f2	g2	h2
a1	b1	c1	d1	e1	f1	g1	h1

To make writing and reading chess fast, each piece is assigned a single letter. In English, we use the abbreviations on the right:

King = K
Queen = Q
Bishop = B
Knight = N
Rook = R
Pawn = the file it's on

We number each set of white and black moves. So, the moves **1. e4 d5** mean that, on his very first move, white pushed the pawn in front of his king forward two squares. Then black pushed the pawn in front of his queen ahead two squares in response. Captures are normally marked with an "x." So the notation **2. exd5** means that white captured the pawn. But you may see notation that doesn't bother with the "x," as in "2. ed5." That's okay too.

Some other examples: **Qh5** means the queen moves to h5. Castling short is written **0-0**, while castling long is **0-0-0**. If you get to play **b8(Q)+** (another way to write the same move is **b8=Q+**), it means that you promoted your b-pawn to a queen and gave check. May all your moves be so powerful!

Another special convention: Although the word "exchange" means to trade, "Exchange" (with a capital "E") means the trade of a knight or bishop for a more-valuable rook. A player who manages this trade "wins the Exchange."

Chess Symbols

There are a number of symbols that chess players use for shorthand when "annotating," or commenting on moves. For example, **13. Rxa6+! +−** means that white made a capture on a6 with his rook, giving check, and that it was a good move, giving white a decisive advantage.

+−	White has a decisive advantage.
±	White has a clear advantage.
±	White has a slight advantage.
=	The chances are equal.
∓	Black has a slight advantage.
∓	Black has a clear advantage.
−+	Black has a decisive advantage.
!!	A very good move
!	A good move
?	A weak move
??	A blunder
!?	An interesting or provocative move, often involving some risk
?!	A dubious move

"You have to learn the rules
of the game.
And then you have to play
better than anyone else."
—Albert Einstein

—Level I—

Lesson Two

How to Win Chess Games

By the end of this lesson, you will know and be able to apply:
* *the four basic winning strategies of chess,*
* *the best methods to begin a chess game, and*
* *three important ideas to keep in mind at every move of a game*

You will also know:
* *when and how a game can be drawn, and*
* *how to recognize the three stages of a chess game.*

In Level I, Lesson One, you learned about the board and pieces. You know all the moves and can play anyone a complete, legal game of chess. But there is, of course, a difference between playing and winning.

Many readers would say that the title of Lesson Two is what it's all about. This lesson, the final one of our Level I, will teach you how to win. Of course you won't learn everything there is to know about winning chess games in this brief lesson, but you'll learn the basics—what we call *The Four Basic Winning Strategies*, and, using them, you will indeed conquer opponents you have never beaten before.

A winning formula

The four basic winning strategies are a sort of algorithm or protocol—a step-by-step formula, to be taken in order. You first try to implement Strategy #1, and if it is not available, go to

The four basic winning strategies are a sort of step-by-step formula, to be taken in order.

#2, and so on. You will be a dangerous opponent who knows how to win chess games!

Developing quick sight of the board through visualization

But before we get to winning strategy #1, you should start practicing a crucial skill. To win chess games, you must also become intimately familiar with the board, not just with how the pieces move. Good chess players quickly notice, in any position, the squares the pieces and pawns can move to. A player who can process this information fast is said to have "quick sight of the board." It's true that practice games build this skill, but even many experienced players are handicapped by poor visualization because they have never used the *best basic exercise* to build up their sight of the board.

Visualizing the board

Close your eyes and practice seeing an empty board in your mind.

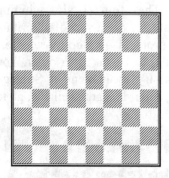

You won't be able to see all

the squares clearly at once. But as you practice, you'll be able to see the parts you focus on clearly. Quiz yourself with questions like these:

• Is the e6-square light or dark?

• Which diagonals cross e6—where do these diagonals begin and end? (For example, one of the two diagonals is h3-c8.)

• What color is each square at the extreme ends (the "top and bottom") of the file (the e-file) the e6-square sits on?

• What color is each square at the extreme ends of the rank (the sixth rank) that the e6-square sits on?

Write your answers down; then check them by looking at an empty board or the diagram at left. Don't be discouraged if you don't do well at first. You will get better and better as you practice. You can be confident that the time you put in on visualizing techniques will pay you large dividends! You'll be much better able to see threats and other possibilities on the chessboard.

Visualizing simple piece movements

Pick a target square (again, without looking at a board)—for example, c4. Visualize it. Now visualize a white knight on a particular square—for example, its home square, g1. In your mind, move the knight to c4 in the fewest moves possible. When you've done that, choose a different target square and visualize the knight on a different starting square. (Check your solutions by using a real board or diagram.) Use other pieces as well, but do this "blindfold" knight exercise frequently to develop quick sight of those tricky horsemen and their surprising threats. That way, you'll be surprised less often in an actual game! Your ultimate goal is to be able to relocate the piece in under 15 seconds.

Make up your own visualization exercises—"chess meditation"

You can do these exercises anyplace and anytime—even waiting in line or lying in bed before you fall asleep. (It can be a very effective way to clear and calm your mind, by the way—a sort of "chess meditation"!)

If you can learn to "see" the board in your mind in this way—and we guarantee you that, with practice, you can—you will let all of your natural talent and knowledge emerge during a game and be able to find the kinds of tactics and formulate the kinds of strategies you will learn in the rest of this book.

Winning chess strategy #1: look for checkmate!

Keep in mind what your ultimate goal is in a chess game—*checkmate*, putting the enemy king in check in a way that it is impossible for him to escape. While playing a game, look first to see if you can checkmate your opponent.

Remember, unless your opponent gives up first, you can never win a chess game, no matter how far ahead you are in material, unless you checkmate the enemy king! All the other tactics and strategies you will learn are preparatory to checkmate. They help make it possible for you to checkmate your opponent or to avoid being checkmated, but they don't in themselves win. So you can see that knowing how to checkmate is supremely important.

Let's look at some basic checkmate patterns at different stages of the game.

Do the 'blindfold' knight exercise frequently to develop quick sight of those tricky horsemen and their surprising threats!

White to move: 1. Qxf7#

Black to move: 1. ... Qh4#

White to move: 1. Qxh7+ Kf8 2. Qh8#
Black to move: 1. ... Qe1#

White to move: 1. Qg7#
Black to move escapes with: 1. ... Qa1+
and 2. ...Qxf6, winning.

White to move: 1. Ra5 (or any waiting
move on the a-file) 1. ... Kc8 2. Ra8#

Winning chess strategy #2: try to win material

We've just seen that checkmate can happen at any stage of the game. Although you certainly don't want to miss a chance to checkmate your opponent during a game, the fact is that most of the time you won't have the opportunity. So what should you do if there's no checkmate possible? Look to see if you can win material. If you have substantially more power on the board, you can eventually force checkmate.

In this part of our lesson, we'll learn what it means to win material and why you should do it. Then we'll look at some of the most common ways to achieve this.

What is "winning material"? The easiest example—and all too common in the games of beginners—is to capture one of your opponent's pieces that he has left carelessly undefended. Chess players love a free piece! Look at the position on the following page, top left. It's your move as white. You are in check. What's your best move?

Check and Checkmate Symbols

+ Remember, a plus or a cross sign after a move indicates check.

The number sign after a move means that move was checkmate!

Look to see if you can win material. If you have substantially more power on the board, you can checkmate.

Can white win a piece?

Black's bishop can capture the enemy bishop on e4, but then white would recapture with his pawn. It's a trade.

Yes, with 1. Bxd4, white takes black's knight and, since black cannot recapture, white remains one piece ahead. Chess players say he is a "piece up." That's a winning advantage.

Trading (exchanging)

Trading pieces is very different from winning a piece, although some beginners confuse these basics. If you take a piece and your opponent can recapture your attacking piece right away, that's a trade (or an exchange). Look at the diagram at the top of the next column.

Here black doesn't "win" a piece; he exchanges pieces of equal value. It's an even swap. That doesn't make it a bad move. But it hasn't won material.

The concept of the material advantage and "trading down"

We need to interrupt our discussion of the four winning stratgies to make sure you understand the importance of trading down when you're ahead. Imagine playing basketball against an evenly-matched team, five players against five players. Then a player on the other team sprains an ankle and has to come off the court, but his team doesn't have a replacement. It's now five against four—a serious advantage for your team. But now suppose that there was a special rule allowing the team remaining with five players to "trade down"—to have each of its players leave the court with one of the other team members until it's two against one. As team captain, you would immediately take advantage of our imaginary rule to maximize winning chances.

The idea in a chess game is much the same. If you get to be a piece up, you want to exchange pieces until your material advantage clearly dominates.

Sometimes just exchanging pieces can win material

You don't have to *win* a piece outright to win material. At the end of Lesson I, we looked at the approximate relative values of the pieces.

     ♛   = 9 points

     ♜   = 5 points

     ♝   = 3 points

     ♞   = 3 points

     ♟   = 1 point

(Since the king can't be captured, his majesty doesn't appear on this scale of values.)

Study this example:

Can white exchange pieces in a way that results in a win of material?

In this position, white can capture black's rook with his bishop. It's true that black can recapture with his king. So is it a trade? Well, it's not an *even* trade, since black's rook is worth more than white's bishop. In fact, chess players have a term for winning material by exchanging a minor piece—a knight or a bishop—for an enemy rook. It's called "winning the Exchange." (Note the capital "E," used to distinguish it from a mere swap.)

Of course, there's another piece-for-piece trade that's even more lopsided.

White to move: Black will exchange his knight for white's queen.

What's the best move for white in this position?

After the white king (which is in check) moves, black will capture white's queen with his knight. The queen is three times as valuable as the knight! Black will have a crushing material advantage.

Pawns are material too!

Our discussion of material force shouldn't leave out even the lowly pawn. Every chessman on the board is "material" and is therefore important. In a game between experts, often winning a single pawn leads to the win of the game!

It is true that sometimes a good player can bait a trap with a "poison" pawn. So you should think before snatching a free pawn. But if you don't see a good reason not to take it, grab it!

With 1. Bxb5, white takes the unprotected pawn and has the superior position, since he is ahead, even though by the smallest possible unit, without drawbacks.

The three basic tactics that win material

Because most of a chess game revolves around each player trying to win material, it's important to get pretty good at spotting how to do this. Chess players call this element of the game *tactics*.

Tactics are the fireworks, and some would say the poetry, of chess. They are the tricks or weapons used to win material—or sometimes to gain some other type of advantage on the chessboard.

You can win material by winning a piece or pawn outright—or by trading one of your pieces for a more valuable one of your opponent's.

A great master once said that "Chess is 99% tactics," and he was making a good point.

Fortunately, the great players of the past have worked out the basic types of tactics to make them easy to learn. This book will teach you many types of tactics, and each has a name to make it easier to remember and talk about. In this lesson, we'll look at the three most common. If you learn these three basic tactics, you will be better than the vast majority of the casual players you meet. Indeed, they will think you win by magic or good luck. (There's no need to enlighten them!)

Tactic #1: the double attack

A double attack does what its name implies—it's a single move that makes two separate threats at one time. Take a look at what the lowly white pawn below is accomplishing.

Even though it's black's move, he must lose a whole piece for a pawn!

This kind of double attack is often called a *pawn fork* (picture an old-fashioned pitch fork with two tines). It is an important trick to remember. The white pawn is attacking two of black's pieces at once. Even though it's black's move, he will lose a piece for a pawn—and would then, with best play, lose by force. Be careful of letting your own pieces fall into an enemy pawn fork!

Every chessman is capable of double attack. Take a look at these examples:

White to move and win a piece

In the position above, white plays 1. Kd3, attacking both black pieces at once, and wins one of them, restoring material equality.

White to move has a double attack.

In the diagram above, white's queen is attacked by black's pawn on g6. But she has a move that double-attacks black's king and rook on h8: 1. Qxe5+!. Black loses his rook.

White's pawn on e5 forks (double-attacks) black's bishop and knight.

Here both the black bishop on d6 and knight on f6 are attacked, and one of them will perish, in exchange for only a pawn: 1. ... Nxe4 2. exd6. Black's attempt to escape from the double attack with 1. ... Bb4+ fails because of 2. c3, when, again, both black pieces are under attack.

Tactic #2: the skewer

In a skewer, a more valuable piece is attacked and forced to move, exposing the less valuable piece behind it to capture. Think of making a shish kebab. You stab a cooking skewer completely through the first delicacy, for example a mushroom, and then push the skewer through another

element, perhaps an onion. The chess tactic takes its name from this process. Take a look at the diagram below.

Shish kebab knight! Black's bishop skewers the knight, which has to move to avoid capture, exposing the pawn on c3.

Queens, rooks and bishops can perform the skewer. Bishops are the most frequent practitioners.

White skewers black's rook on the 8th rank.

The black king, in the position above, must move off the

If you learn the basic tactics, you will be better than the vast majority of casual players you meet!

Because most of a chess game revolves around each player trying to win material, it's important for you to get good at tactics!

back rank, and white will capture black's rook on a8.

Use the skewer idea from the previous diagram to find a win for white, on move.

As white, if you know how to use the skewer, you can rattle off a win in a typical position above. 1. Rh8!. Now you threaten to promote your pawn with 2. a8(Q), which would be protected by your rook. If that happens, black would have nothing better than to give up his own rook for the new queen, leaving white with an extra rook, with which he could force mate. So black must play 1. ... Rxa7. Here's the new position:

White plays 2. Rh7+ and wins black's rook.

Now look at the one-mover below.

White wins the Exchange using the skewer.

White plays 1. Bd5!+, and when the black king moves, white continues 2. Bxg8, evening material, winning black's rook for the bishop.

Chess players have a saying: "Pin it and win it!" But not every pin wins material.

Tactic #3: the pin

The pin is the most common tactic, occurring in nearly every game at least once. It's the flip side of the skewer. The pinning piece attacks one of two enemy pieces along the same rank or file. The enemy piece in front can't move without exposing the piece behind it—normally the more *valuable* piece.

Don't move that knight!

Above, black's bishop pins the knight, which can't move without exposing the valuable white queen to capture.

Queens, rooks and bishops can pin other pieces. Bishops are again the most likely to use the tactic.

White to move: Multiple choice:
A. 1. Bb3 or B. 1. Bf3

The answer is "B." That move not only attacks the pawn on d5 but also *pins* it against the knight.

In this next position, black has a pin that he can exploit to win material. How does he do that?

Black to move:
Use the pin to win the knight.

Black attacks the pinned piece with 1. ... e4!. If the knight on f3 moves, black wins the rook. If the knight stays put, black will capture it with 2. ... exf3.

Chess players have a saying, "Pin it and win it!" Not every pin wins material, however. But pins have to be paid attention to! Look carefully at this position.

Black to move:
Can black save the knight?

If it were white's move, of

course he would play 1. e4!, winning the knight. But since it's black's move, and he's noticed the coming threat to his pinned knight, he plays 1. ... Rd7, ready to meet 2. e4 with 2. ... Nf6 (notice that the knight protects the rook).

When a chessman is pinned to its king, of course it's illegal for the pinned piece to move! Such a pin is called an *absolute* pin.

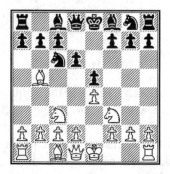

The white bishop establishes an absolute pin on the black knight.

Winning chess strategy #3: improve your position

If you can't checkmate your opponent, and you don't see a way to win material, you should *improve your position*. (Good things come to good positions!) Improving your position moves us from the arena of tactics to that of true strategy—long-term planning, as opposed to the short-term tactics.

One of the most effective ways to improve your position is to examine each of your pieces and see if it can be put on a square that gives it more influence—to control more, or more important, squares. Take a look at the position below.

White can't mate or win material, so he improves his position.

White uses his move to reposition an important piece. He moves his rook to c1—getting it to an open file, where the power of the rook is felt all the way across the board in the enemy's camp. The move also restricts the black rook, which is now prevented from taking control of the only open file.

Take a look at the following positions to see if you can pick out a move in each that would improve the effectiveness of a piece in a way that improves your overall position.

Besides improving the effectiveness of one of your pieces, another way to improve your position is to make your *opponent's* position *worse*.

Black plays 1. ... h3, making white's
position worse by imprisoning his bishop.

The next two diagrams take
you through an opening
sequence in which black makes
good moves by having an eye
toward improving his position.

After 1. e4 d5 2. e5

Black knows to bring his
bishop out before playing ... e6,
so that it gets *outside* the pawn
chain. So he could play 2. ... Bf5,
or first 2. ... c5; for example: 2. ...
c5 3. c3 Nc6 4. Nf3 and now 4. ...
Bf5 or 4. ... Bg4, when black's
light-square bishop is active in
the game.

Black has avoided locking in his light-
square bishop and has an active game.

In this next position, white
can grab a pawn or make a move
that gives him a dominating position. What should he choose?

What's white's best move?

White should eschew capturing the pawn and instead play
1. Bd5!, restricting black's
knight. White will then win the
horseman with 2. b4. This is
another case showing that handi-
capping your opponent's pieces
can be as good as improving your
own!

Winning chess strategy #4: pawn promotion

The final winning strategy
we'll see in this lesson is pawn
promotion. You learned the rule
of pawn promotion in Lesson
One: if your pawn reaches the
other side of the board, it can be
promoted, normally to a power-

ful queen. Many chess games between evenly matched players boil down to an endgame with few if any pieces. To win, one side must promote one of his remaining pawns. (This wonderful rule allows revitalizing the game by adding back power to the board.)

Take a look at this position:

How does white, to move, promote his pawn?

After 1. d7 Ke7 2. Kc7, black cannot stop the pawn from reaching the back rank and queening. Then white's overwhelming material advantage will make it easy to checkmate black.

When a chess game can't be won

A chess game doesn't always produce a winner and a loser. And that's how it should be. Sometimes players are evenly matched, both playing a careful and logical game. Sometimes the mistakes simply even out! You've seen how chessgames

can be won. Let's look at how they can be drawn.

1. Insufficient mating material

If so much material is traded off that neither side remains with a sufficient force to checkmate, it's a draw.

Black's king cannot be checkmated by white's king and bishop. It's a draw!

Of course, if white had a pawn instead of a bishop, it would not be a draw by insufficient mating material, since there would be a possibility of the pawn being promoted.

2. Stalemate

We quickly covered this possibility in Lesson One. If one side has no legal moves but its king is not in check, the game ends in a special kind of a draw (but a draw nevertheless), called *stalemate*. This happens only late in the game when there aren't many pieces left on the board.

It's black's turn. He's not in check but has no legal move. It's a draw by stalemate!

3. Three-time repetition of position

If exactly the same position is repeated for the third time under identical conditions, the player on move has the right (but not the obligation) to claim a draw. This is obviously a good rule, because otherwise one player could keep returning to the identical position over and over, without making progress, and waste everyone's time. Sometimes knowing this rule can save you half a point, as you may draw a game you are losing because your opponent gets careless and allows the three-time repetition of a position.

The rule does not require the position to be repeated *three times in a row* (a frequent misunderstanding). The rule applies to the third time an identical position is reached any time in a game, even if the occurrences are separated by several, or even many, moves. (You can see why

sometimes one player falls into a draw this way unexpectedly.)

In addition to all the pieces and pawns being in the same position, all conditions have to be identical in all three positions. This can be the trickiest part. For example, the same player has to be on move; the rights to castle have to be the same; the pawns' options to capture *en passant* have to be the same.

White, way behind in material, can force a three-time repetition to claim a draw.

Above, play would go: 1. ... Kh8 2. Qh6+ Kg8 3. Qg6+ (twice in the same position) 3. ... Kh8 4. Qg6+ (three time repetition), when white claims a draw before actually making the last move. (To claim a draw by three-time repetition, you must have kept a score of the game. We've shown how to do this at the very end of Level I, Lesson 1.)

4. Fifty-move rule

If no pawn has been moved, nor any capture has been made in 50 moves, either side can claim a draw. Again, this good rule prevents endless "piece shuffling" that doesn't get anywhere. (Claiming a draw with the 50-move rule also requires that at least one of the players keeps score.)

5. Perpetual check

This is really an idea and a useful term whose conditions can fall under numbers 3 and 4 above. Sometimes it is obvious that one player can keep checking his opponent forever, without giving mate. When that happens, the players call it a draw, rather than waiting for 50 moves or a three-time repetition.

Black to move:
Which pawn should he queen?

After 1. ... e1(Q)? 2. Qe6+ Kf8 3. Qf6+, perpetual check.

Black avoids this with 1. ... d1(Q), after which, black should win.

6. Agreement

At any time, the two opponents may shake hands and agree to a draw. But it is considered unsportsmanlike not to make a real fight. This rule is useful because it can save time in what experienced players call "dead-drawn" positions. But we recommend that, for now, you play your practice games out to checkmate or until there is insufficient mating material.

Three stages of a chess game

A chess game that goes on for a long fight generally goes through three stages. It's often useful to be able to tell what stage a game is in.

Opening: the first stage, in which a pawn or two is moved, and some pieces are *developed* (getting off their home squares).

Middlegame: the second stage, after the opening, that generally begins somewhere between the eighth and the twelfth move.

*Endgame (*sometimes called the *ending)*: the final stage, when

In the opening, move one or two pawns so that they either occupy or control the center.

In the opening, develop your pieces, knights and bishops first, and then castle.

only a few pieces remain on the board—the opposing queens have likely been exchanged—and the play centers around pawn *promotion*. The kings come out of hiding to help.

How to open a chess game: three winning strategies

You'll learn more about the three stages of a game as you progress through this book. Let's begin by taking a look at what you should do in the opening, at the start of the game.

1. *Take the center*

The four squares in the very middle of the board, e4, d4, e5, and d5, are called the *center*.

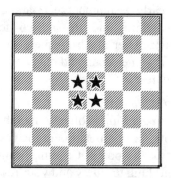

The center squares

Ancient armies readying for a battle jockeyed for the high ground of the battlefield, ideally a hill, because enemy troops would have to waste energy climbing to attack. Additionally, the army arrayed on the high ground knew that their spears and arrows would go farther than their enemy's. Think of the center squares as the high ground of the chessboard. Experienced chess players know that, from the very first moves, the dueling armies must compete for control, if not outright occupation, of the center.

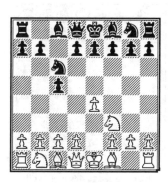

The early battle for the center

White's pawn *occupies* a center square, e4, and *controls* d5 (and f5, a square near the center). Black's pawn on c5 exerts control on d4. White's knight on f3 contests control of d4 while controlling e5, and black's knight on c6 contests d4 and e5.

2. Develop your pieces

Staying with our battlefield analogy, we can say that, at the beginning of the game, both armies are in their barracks. Unless you get your men in battle formation quickly, they can be caught with their backs against the wall (the edge of the board), where they have no mobility and cannot coordinate their movements—a massacre would result. And, like any effective battlefield commander, a strong chess player makes sure all of his troops are effectively placed for the fight. He doesn't attack a well-coordinated major force with a few men. That would waste time and resources.

Black failed to develop, while white took the center and got his pieces into play quickly.

The players reached this position with these moves: 1. e4 a5 (Beginners sometimes try to get their rooks out too soon.) 2. d4 a4 (2. ... Ra6 doesn't work because of 3. Bxa6.) 3. Nf3 Ra5

4. Bd2 Rh5.

Now white can win material with 5. g4!. Black has spent all of his time getting his rook into a trap!

So, in the opening, play one or two pawns to affect the center, and then develop your pieces, knights and bishops first, and castle.

Here both sides have brought out their pieces sensibly to start the game.

In the diagram above, you'll notice that the knights often find an early assignment at f3 and c3 for white, and f6 and c6 for black. After all, from there they control the center and many other squares.

3. Castle early

Your king is often vulnerable at its starting position in the center of the board. Castling brings your king to safety and your rook into play. Castle early!

Three final pieces of move-by-move advice

You're ready to take on anyone. The more games you play, the better you'll get—so play at every opportunity. Don't be afraid of losing—but make sure you learn from your losses!

We'll close Level I with three time-tested pieces of advice.

1. Study your opponent's last move carefully!

Every time your opponent makes a move, call a time out in your head. Don't respond automatically. Study the piece or pawn he has moved in its new location. Can it be captured or exchanged for a less valuable man? Where can it go that it couldn't before? Follow the lines it can now move along. What does it threaten? Is it poised to capture one of your pieces? Does it attack your king or otherwise threaten his safety? Or perhaps your opponent's last move creates new opportunities for you.

Our #1 is the most important single piece of chess advice anyone can ever give you!

2. Look twice, move once!

Careful carpenters have the motto, "Measure twice, cut once"—a great caution to adapt to chess. Just like a saw-cut that makes the board too short, a bad move can't be taken back!

So, before you touch the piece you think you want to move, examine that "candidate move" carefully in your mind's eye. Imagine it on its new square. Can it be taken for free? If it is defended, can it be captured by a less valuable piece? What new threats would your opponent have once you play the move you have in mind? Does it open important lines, for example?

3. Keep your king safe!

At all times, watch out for your king. Think of yourself as having the responsibilities of a busy babysitter. Sure, there are many other things to do in the house, but first of all you must keep all harm from your vulnerable charge. (After he grows up a bit, your king can walk into the endgame fray—but he still may need a bit of looking after.)

Happy chess!

Level I, Lesson Two
Memory Markers!

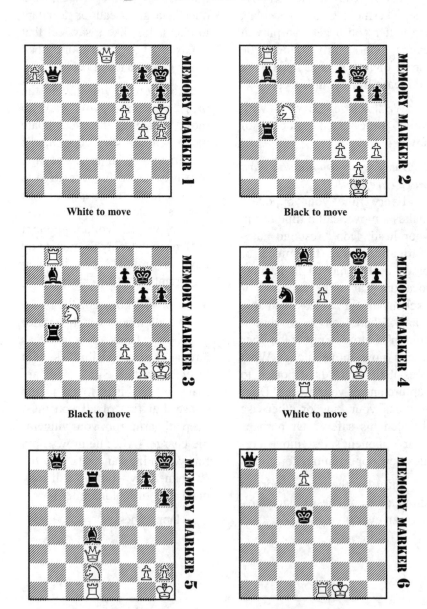

MEMORY MARKER 1

White to move

MEMORY MARKER 2

Black to move

MEMORY MARKER 3

Black to move

MEMORY MARKER 4

White to move

MEMORY MARKER 5

White to move

MEMORY MARKER 6

White to move

Solutions:

MM1: **1. a8=B!** (If 1. a8=Q or 1. a8=R, then 1. ... Qf7+, forcing stalemate.) **1. ... Qb3** (to stop 2. Bd5) **2. Qd7** (white insists, and wins).

MM2: Black gets out of the pin with **1. ... Rb1+ 2. Kh2 Be4**.

MM3: Black loses a pinned piece, but not necessarily the game:
1. ... Rb5!!, forcing **2. Nxb7**. White is up a piece, but black's pin immobilizes both of white's pieces. To unpin, white will have to bring his king to c6 (to support the knight), in a process that will lose at least two pawns, with a likely draw.

MM4: **1. Rxd8+ Nxd8 2. e7**, and white wins, because he threatens both 3. exd8=Q+, and 3. e8=Q+ (if the black knight could disappear, black would have won with 2. ... Kf7).

MM5: **1. Nf3** wins the pinned bishop and the game. If, however, 1. Nb3, black turns that pin into a deadly discovered attack:1. ... Bg1, and black wins. Note that 1. ... Bg1 is also a double-attack—that is, an attack on two targets.

MM6: **1. d8=Q+ Qxd8 2. Rd1+.** This skewer wins the queen, and the game. Reversing the move order with 1. Rd1+ leads only to a draw: 1. ... Ke5 2. d8=Q Qf3+, with a perpetual check.

—Level II—
Getting Tournament Tough

Level One showed you the basics of winning chess, giving you enough information to be your local neighborhood and coffee-shop champion—unless there is an experienced tournament player on the block. Tournament players are a special group who move the bar considerably higher. Most any tournament player can beat most non-tournament players. Think of the neighborhood baseball player who stars in local pick-up games. He or she knows the basics and has some good moves. But then think of someone who's come up through organized teams and perhaps even plays in the minor leagues. That player is simply on a different level.

The good news is that you: (a) don't have to wear a uniform, and (b) don't have to spend the hundreds of hours athletes must put in simply to get into the kind of physical condition required to compete at high levels in sports. Instead you can concentrate on acquiring the knowledge and technique you need. (It is helpful to be in reasonably good shape. A tough chess game requires a surprising amount of physical as well as mental stamina. And, by the way, did you know that while learning and thinking hard, your brain uses 15 times as many calories—nearly 100 per hour—as it does passively zoning out in front of the TV?)

You're busy and you catch on quickly. Our job in Level II is to give you only the practical, game-winning information required to get to a tournament-competitive level of skill. We'll cut through the mysteries of strategy and tactics to show you just what you need to know. We won't waste your time asking you to study rare, one-in-a-thousand-game scenarios. If you focus on the material in this level and continue to practice in the ways we suggest, you will soon reach a level of skill that will make you competitive in official tournaments.

—Level II—

Lesson Three

When a King Is Home Alone

In this lesson, you will learn that it is easy to checkmate the lonely king!

A s we launch into a new level of chess, getting you ready to play against others who read books on the game, we want to remind you to play many practice games of your own. Perhaps one of your current chess partners wants to make the move to Level II with you. It helps to have a training and study partner. You get the benefit of another brain studying a position. And you get invaluable knowledge about how potential opponents react to challenges on the board.

Additionally, a chess partner offers the same advantages as a jogging or gym partner—you get additional motivation to do the workout, and it's a lot more fun with company! For more about finding practice partners, see page 58, "Join a Chess Club!"

To get you to the next level, we need to back up a little bit. You already know that checkmate is the ultimate goal of a chess game. Let's make sure you're confident about how to execute checkmate once you've

All you need to mate a lone king is just one major piece, your own king— and some basic knowledge!

won a healthy amount of material. Nothing is more embarrassing to a serious player than playing well to reach an easy win—and then not being able to close the deal!

Checkmate with queen and king against a lone king

It always takes at least two chessmen to mate. The easiest is with king and queen. These mates are common and easy to learn. It's true that the powerful queen can, by herself, drive the enemy king to the edge of the board, but she cannot force checkmate. By herself, she can only force stalemate.

White to move and checkmate

1. Qg4 Kd5 2. Qf4 Kc5 3. Qe4 Kd6

Whichever way the black king falls back, the queen continues to cut the part of the board he falls back to into smaller and smaller pieces. For example, if instead   3. … Kb5 4. Qd4 Ka5

5. Qb2 Ka4 6. Qb6 Ka3 7. Qb5 (even faster is 7. Kf3, going for the kill) 7. … Ka2 8. Qb4.

Black can choose only which edge of the board he is forced to.

4. Qf5 Kc6 5. Qe5 Kd7 6. Qf6 Kc7 7. Qe6 Kb7 8. Qd6 Ka7 9. Qc6 Kb8 10. Qd7 Ka8

Caution! Stalemate zone!

Now you have to be careful. Notice that cutting off another square with 11. Qc7?? produces stalemate. That's not the result you should want a queen up! You must allow the enemy king two squares to shuffle back and forth on while you bring up your king. You can mate in five moves— four to get your king to at least c6, and one to mate:

11. Kf3 Kb8 12. Ke4 Ka8

Black has no other choices!

13. Kd5 Kb8 14. Kc6 Ka8 15. Qb7#

One of the possible mates against a lone king facing king and queen.

Using the queen to first corral the king toward the edge is certainly one method to use to execute this mate. But notice it took 15 moves. Let's look at the most efficient way, getting your king into the act right away.

Using your king from the beginning.

1. Kf3 Kf5 2. Qd5+ Kg6 3. Kf4 Kf6 4. Qd6+ Kf7 5. Kg5 Kg7

The black king is running out of territory.

6. Qf6+

This way takes one move longer than a perfect solution. But you don't have to be perfect to win this ending. For your information, white mates most quickly with: 6. Qe7+ Kg8 7. Kg6 Kh8 8. Qg7#.

6. ... Kg8

Remember, king and queen can't checkmate, or, importantly, can't stalemate the lonely king except on the very edge of the board. So with the opponent's king on the edge, be careful!

7. Qe7

With your queen on the sixth rank and the black king on the eighth, there are plenty of stalemates to avoid, for example, 7. Kg6? and 7. Kh6?.

7. ... Kh8 8. Kg6 Kg8

Practice checkmating the black king, no matter which edge of the board he runs to—he can choose his poison, but he must drink it! Initially, this should take you no more than 20 moves for each mate, in under 10 minutes. Keep practicing until you checkmate in less than 15 moves and under two minutes—with no stalemates!

9. Qg7#

The black king is checkmated.

King and rook versus king

This is another quite common, basic checkmate that you should know. The king and rook against a lone king can force checkmate easily. Because the rook is less powerful than the queen, the process takes a few more moves, but once you catch onto the basic method, you should have no trouble checkmating your opponent in a real game in which you have this material advantage.

Let's look at a starting position in which the defending king is near the middle of the board—his best defensive position. We need to force the king to the edge.

Don't try to memorize the moves. Remember the method.

White to move and checkmate.

1. Rg4!

You know that a "!" after a move means it's the best choice. Why is this move so good? It's not hard to see that, in one stroke, it cuts off the enemy king from half the board! If you chose 1. Rd2 for the same reason, then also give yourself an "!"—we won't worry about which move checkmates a bit faster—mate is mate!

1. ... Kb5

Black must give ground, backing toward one edge of the board or the other. (If black chooses a slightly different path with 1. ... Kc6, white continues to reduce his options with 2. Rc4+ Kb6 3. Kd5.)

2. Kd6 Kb6 3. Rb4+ Ka5 4. Kc5

Don't try to memorize the moves.
Remember the method.

In just a few moves, black has been forced to the edge!

4. ... Ka6 5. Kc6

Black has been forced to the edge.

Notice that if it were white's move again, 6. Ra4 would be checkmate!

5. ... Ka7

If 5. ... Ka5, then 6. Rc4 (or anyplace on the fourth rank except a4, where the rook could be captured), and black must play into 6. ... Ka6, 7. Ra4#).

6. Rb1

There are many ways to mate—this one is the fastest. Notice that it is a waiting move, giving the turn to black and forcing him to be mated immediately on a6 or move to the corner square.

6. ... Ka8 7. Kc7

White puts his king on the right square to mate when black makes his next forced move.

7. ... Ka7 8. Ra1#

Using an empty board, set this ending up in various positions, with the superior side to move and force mate. Practice against a friend or yourself, making the best moves you can for the weaker side. Pay attention to the three-part method:

1. Cut off the board.

2. Force the enemy king to the edge.

3. If needed, play a waiting move with your rook to force a mating position.

Your ultimate goal is to be able to force checkmate from any position in three minutes and less than 20 moves.

King and queen against king and bishop

The queen is so powerful that, with the help of her king, she can force checkmate even when the enemy king has a minor piece on his side. The winning method is actually very similar to king and queen versus the lone king.

The king and queen can force mate
against a king and minor piece.

The queen stays on the squares
not covered by the enemy bishop.

Two tips for the superior side:

1. Stay off squares the enemy bishop can cover.

2. If the defending side gives away or loses his extra piece, take it—the mate is then a simple case of queen and king versus lone king, which we've already covered.

1. Ke2

The slow-moving king must be brought into the action sooner or later.

1. ... Bf6

To be checkmated, the black king must be driven to one of the edges of the board, so his highness is in no hurry to give ground.

2. Kf3 Be5 3. Ke4 Bf6 4. Qd5+

White's king has advanced on the enemy as far as he can, and now supports the queen as she moves up, cutting off the board and pushing the enemy king back. From now on, she will stay only on the light squares, making the enemy bishop ineffective.

4. ... Ke7 5. Kf5 Bg7 6. Qe6+ Kd8

If 6. ... Kf8, running to the shorter side of the board, the mate is faster. After 7. Kg6 (notice that this position would be stalemate if black didn't have a bishop to move), mate follows with 8. Qf7.

After black's **6. ... Kd8**, the practical move is **7. Qg8+**, winning the bishop with a double attack, making it the easy queen-and-king versus lone king ending we've already gone over. Most tournament players would make this choice. However, for the record, the fastest mate ignores the win of material: 7. Qc6 Ke7 8.Qc7+ Kf8 9. Kg6 Bb2 10. Qd8# (or 10. Qf7#).

Checkmate, while the bishop looks on helplessly.

King and queen against king and knight

In this ending, once again, the stronger side still wins wherever the pieces are positioned, but of course it's a bit trickier, because the knight always threatens a surprise. The attacker must be careful never to fall into a fork. The defender, for his part, must look out for a double attack that wins the knight, making the checkmate easier.

The queen and king can force mate as well. But look out for forks!

1. Qe6+ Kg7 2. Kg4 Nh6+ 3. Kh5 Ng8 4. Kg5 Kf8 5. Qd7

Ne7 6. Kf6 Ng8+ 7. Ke6

7. ... Ne7

If 7. ... Nh6 8. Qh7 Ke8 (8. ... Ng4 9. Qf7#) 9. Qe7#.

8. Qxe7+ Kg8 9. Kf6 Kh8 10. Qg7#

Go over the examples in this chapter a few times to get the mating techniques down pat, and you'll be ready to give the *coup de grace* to anyone you've won major material from.

Join a Chess Club!

Practice is crucial at every stage of your chess development. It's important to play many practice games as you go through this book. And you'll need a higher level and a wider circle of competition to progress at Level II. So one of the most important things you can do at this stage is to find a local chess club.

Many community libraries host a weekly club. So do many schools. The clubs that involve the most serious and best players are affiliated with the national chess federation of the country you live in. The U.S. Chess Federation has hundreds of official clubs across America. You can find which club is nearest you by going online to its website to look at state-by-state listings of official clubs. The Chess Federation of Canada and the English Chess Federation are also well organized. You'll find your local club welcoming and membership inexpensive. If, when visiting, you decide you're not yet ready to play, watch for a few meetings and sit in on post-game analysis by the players. You'll quickly learn who the club champions are. Listen carefully to them when they give advice or are going over one of their games. But, most importantly, try to meet, observe, and play members who are closer to your own level.

Both of the authors began to get serious about chess by joining local chess clubs. Besides improving your chess at a club, you'll meet interesting people. And chess clubs may be among the most democratic gatherings on Earth. We've witnessed CEOs of large companies asking advice on a move from a retired maintenance worker, and young students checkmating professors.

There are also a number of very fine online clubs. Although we highly recommend the benefit you'll receive from interacting with other people face-to-face, there is no doubt that the easy availability of online play at a moment's notice, without even leaving your favorite chair, makes high-quality practice much more accessible. And the best online clubs offer online instructional videos and other tutoring.

To find real and virtual chess clubs, and lots of other information, go to the United States Chess Federation's official website: www.uschess.org. Or call them at 931-787-1234. Not in the U.S.? It's still easy. Just go to the World Chess Federation's site: www.fide.com. Click on "Member Federations" to find your nation's home page.

Level I, Lesson Two
Memory Markers!

MEMORY MARKER 1

Black to move

MEMORY MARKER 2

White to move

MEMORY MARKER 3

White to move

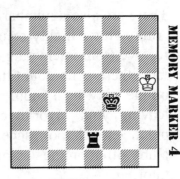

MEMORY MARKER 4

Black to move

MEMORY MARKER 5

Black to move

MEMORY MARKER 6

White to move

Solutions:

MM1: The lonely queen normally wins against the lonely rook, although not easily, by first driving the enemy king to the edge. This position is an example of why it's not always easy: stalemate!

1. ... Rg7+. Now if 2. Kf5, 2. ... Rf7; and if 2. Kh6, 2. ... Rh7+ 3. Kg6 Rh6+ 4. Kxh6, stalemate.

MM2: Careful! All the king's moves, as well as 1. Qd7, lead to an immediate draw via stalemate. White wins by **1. Qd6+ Kf7 2. Kh6 Ke8 3. Qc7 Kf8 4. Kg6**, and checkmates in two moves. Also good is thematic 1. Qf6+ Ke8 2. Qg7 (7th rank cutoff), then bringing the white king around for a checkmate.

MM3: 1. Qb7, followed by the white king's march.

MM4: 1. ... Re6 2. Kh4 Rh6#

MM5: 1. ... Bf7, forcing a draw.

MM6: **1. Kf5** (not 1. Kg6 or 1. Ke6, which would be met by a fork, 1. ... Nf8+) **1. ... Nf8 2. Qa7** (away from fork) **2. ... Nh7 3. Kg6 Nf8+ 4. Kh6**, winning.

**"If we do not hang together,
we will hang separately."
—Benjamin Franklin**

—Level II—

Lesson Four

The Chessmen at Work

In this lesson, you will learn how the chessmen can work individually and together—sometimes in surprising ways!

We have already seen many examples of what each chessman can accomplish. Each of them can double-attack. Because the queen and the knight can strike in up to eight directions, these two are the most dangerous multiple-attackers.

Bishops, rooks and queens can skewer, Xray, and pin. Knights can leap over defensive barriers. In fact, such barriers can even become self-suffocating to the defender, as in the example of a smothered mate on page 72.

Pawns can be turned into queens, or, occasionally, under-promoted to a different piece.

In this chapter, we'll concentrate on how certain groups of chessmen (usually in pairs) work together.

We divide our examples into six sections: rook and bishop, bishop and knight, queen and bishop, rook and knight, queen and knight, and pawns by themselves.

These examples will give you a good "feel" for how the chessmen can cooperate!

These examples will give you a good feel for how the chessmen can cooperate!

Rook and bishop

Study the diagram below, and before going beyond it, see if you can find how white, on move, checkmates black in one move.

Checkmate in the corner

White plays **1. Ra8!**, and the black monarch, part of his remaining army only a hindrance, finds himself checkmated!

The windmill

The position at the top of the next column is from a famous game in 1925. The Mexican master Carlos Torre is on move as white against Emanuel Lasker. White's bishop is pinned against his queen by black's queen on b5, and at the same time, the bishop is under attack by black's pawn on h6. Is Torre in trouble? (By the way, white's opponent is a former world champion and one of the all-time greats.)

White to move. Is he in trouble?

Torre, who has foreseen the position, uncorks the one brilliant move that saves him—and even forces a win!

1. Bf6!!

White ignores the pin and leaves his queen *en prise*! Black has nothing better than to take it.

1. ... Qxh5 2. Rxg7+ Kh8

White to move: He will unleash a discovered check!

Now we can see white's idea. Because black's king is boxed in, white has been able to set up what chess players came to call "the windmill." His rook will move with *discovered check*, making it immune to capture.

When you execute a discovered check, you move one piece and in so doing uncover another of your pieces lurking behind it that gives check to the enemy king. This is a powerful tactic!

3. Rxf7+ Kg8

The only move. The king will be forced back to h8, *reloading* the discovered check!

4. Rg7+ Kh8 5. Rxb7+ Kg8 6. Rg7+ Kh8

White has collected enough booty with his windmill. Now it's time to win back the queen.

7. Rg5+

White has used the windmill to just about clear out the seventh rank. Now he goes after the queen.

7. ... Kh7 8. Rxh5 Kg6!

This is clearly black's best move, double-attacking white's rook and bishop, winning back a piece. But white now has material to spare.

9. Rh3 Kxf6 10. Rxh6+

Although the piece-count is even, white is three pawns up. At the tournament level, that makes it hopeless for black. Go over this game fragment until you clearly understand the process of "the windmill"—using the discovered check to win material, returning to the starting position with check, and then using the discovered check again.

You can see that the white rook gets a free move each time it gets this position (white rook on g7, black king on h8), and it can "reload" this position at will as long as it stays on the seventh rank or on the g-file.

Bishop and knight

In our next example, black is way ahead in material—he's up a whole queen and an Exchange! But it's white's move, and his knight comes pre-loaded with a discovered check, which can be turned into a *double* check!

Suffocation mate!
White to move and mate in two.

1. Nxf7++ Kg8 2. Nh6#

The knight attacks the king

while at the same time controlling the light-square f7. The white bishop controls the dark squares g7 and h8. A black rook blocks the king on f8, and a black pawn blocks His Majesty on h7. Remember this mating pattern!

The black king is suffocated!

Queen and bishop

Pedro Damiano was a Portuguese player of the sixteenth century who wrote a book on chess that was very popular in his day. For some reason, perhaps because of a game he wrote about that used this mating blueprint, his name stuck to a specific mating maneuver. Before we look at it in action, keep this simple mating pattern in your mind. It's a bit like knowing how a mystery yarn ends before you read it.

The End!

Now let's go back to the beginning of the story.

**Damiano's Mate:
White to move and mate
in four moves!**

White is an Exchange down, but it's his move, and black's king lacks protection. To solve this one, you'll need to make use of several techniques that you've already learned—check and discovered check.

1. Bh7+ Kh8

White has "loaded" a discovered check. Can you see how to get from here to the final pattern? Notice that black's rook and queen don't protect any of the three squares in front of black's king: f7, g7, h7.

2. Bg6+! Kg8 3. Qh7+ Kf8 4. Qxf7#

All three of black's king moves were forced—each one was his only move. So, from the beginning it was mate in four. It should be clear now that you will win many more games if you know key basic patterns in which the pieces work together effectively.

Criss-Cross Mate

The powerful queen and bishop can work together in many dangerous ways. Notice in the diagram below that white's queen is under attack from black's bishop. Our immediate reaction may be to move the queen out of danger. But let's take a deep breath and look a bit closer.

We can see that the queen, even though under attack, controls all but one square that the black king can move to. Can you find the mate in one?

White to move—his queen is attacked.
What should he do?

1. Ba6#

Through a combination of resisting our immediate impulse and knowing the mating pattern, we have checkmated black.

Boden's mate

Our next example in this section on queens and bishops working together shows another powerful combination bringing checkmate to a complacent defender. It's named after Samuel Boden, who won a game with this pattern in London in 1853. While there is no need to memorize names like Boden's mate or the Windmill, some players find them helpful.

It's white's move. Everything looks under control, but ...

White to move:
Should black's king feel safe?

1. Qxc6+!! bxc6

The only move.

2. Ba6#

The bishops give a criss-cross mate!

The battery

In the position below, black's queen and bishop form a powerful *battery*. But if black plays 1. ... Qh2+, white's king simply moves to f1. Can you find a preparatory move that "charges" this battery to give a lethal jolt?

Black to move.

How can he "charge" his battery?

1. ... Rh1+! 2. Kxh1 Qxh2#

Rook and knight

Now we'll look at how the rook and knight can cooperate in some lethal ways.

Hook mate

In the following position, black is in check and must decide on one of two possible king moves—one leading to instant

checkmate and one to a roughly equal game.

Black faces a crucial choice.

Black has two moves, marked by the "Xs." One move gives him an equal game, while the other leads to a quick death.

Look what happens if he makes the wrong move:

1. ... Kg7?? 2. Rg8#

Black is mated in the fish-hook pattern.

White's knight and rook suggest the shape of a fishing hook, giving this mating pattern its name. It's crucial that the knight be protected, as it is here, by a diagonally moving chessman, so that the king can't escape by simply capturing the horseman, and so that the only flight square (in this example, h6) not covered by the knight and rook is guarded. Notice also that this mate does not have to take place on the edge of the board.

Of course, the correct move for black in the initial diagram (at the top of the right-hand column on the previous page) is **1. ... Ke7**.

Corner mate

The knight and rook can work together to produce a number of mating patterns. Look at the basic corner mate:

Black is jammed in the corner and checkmated.

Now take a look at this game position with black to move:

Black to move and avoid the corner mate.

Suppose, for example, that black here attacked the white knight with 1. ... Be5. Think back to the corner mate pattern, and you can see that 2. Rg8+ forces checkmate. White sacrifices a rook so that he could play the critical mating move: 2. ... Rxg8 3. Nf7#.

Black actually played **1. ... h6!**, with an approximately equal game. With the h-pawn one square up on h6, if white now plays 2. Rg8+??, black would take the rook, then simply scoot his king up and out of check, say "thank you for the rook," and enjoy an easily won game.

The perpetual check machine

The knight and rook can sometimes set up a mechanism that forces a perpetual check. In the next position, white's two pawns on the seventh rank are poised to force promotion of a queen—if that happened, it would be a sure loss for black. His only hope is a perpetual check.

Black's knight and rook can force a perpetual check.

1. ... Nf3+ 2. Kf1

Not 2. Kh1 Rh2# (This mating pattern has a name too: the Arabian mate.)

The pure pattern of the Arabian mate—white avoids this catastrophe.

2. ... Rd2! 3. b8(Q) Nh2+ 4. Ke1 Nf3+

With black's rook on d2, white's king can't cross the d-file.

5. Kf1 Nh2+ 6. Kg1 Nf3+

Note that neither the f3- nor h2-squares are controlled by white.

The knight and rook have forced a perpetual check.

White must call it a draw by perpetual or walk into mate on h1. From the beginning diagram, a great save for black—made possible because he knew the drawing pattern.

Mind over matter

The great American player-turned-psychologist Reuben Fine wrote that the possibility of a combination—a series of moves, usually involving a sacrifice, that may suddenly turn an equal-looking position into a win—is what makes chess "more than a lifeless mathematical exercise." Combinations, he said, "are the poetry of the game ... They represent the triumph of mind over matter!"

It's black's move in the position at the top of the next column. If he knows the proper mating pattern, he can unleash a lightning bolt from a seemingly blue sky!

Black to move. One preparatory move—then a shocker!

1. ... Ne2+ 2. Kh1

So far, things appear under control for white. His king is tucked behind a friendly three-pawn wall. But white's queen is off on a royal holiday, and black's pieces are perfectly placed to checkmate!

2. ... Qxh2+!! 3. Kxh2

White had no option.

3. ... Rh4#

Another rook-and-knight mate to remember!

Multiple checkmate threats

When you can threaten immediate checkmate with two different moves at once, your opponent can feel like he's been caught walking against the stoplight during rush-hour traffic.

Examine these two new checkmating patterns showing how the rook, knight, and pawn can work together:

Now examine the following endgame, in which black is ahead a piece for a pawn, but it's white's move.

White to move: Can you see how to threaten two mates at once?

1. g6!

After this little pawn-push, it's hopeless for black. White simultaneously threatens two different mates: **2. g7#** and **2. Rf7#**. Because black's pieces are poorly placed for the defense, he can't stop both threats.

Queen and knight

The queen and knight, so different in their movements and capabilities, can also complement each other very effectively.

White to move and force mate in four.

1. Nf7+ Kg8 2. Nh6++ Kh8 (if 2. ... Kf8, 3. Qf7#) **3. Qg8+! Rxg8 4. Nf7#**

Smothered mate!

Pawn teamwork

The lowly pawns can work as a team too.

Pawns and Zugzwang

Zugzwang is a German word (literally meaning "forced move") that chess players use to indicate the obligation to move when you'd prefer not to. But isn't having the move a good thing? Well, although that's usually true, there are times when it would be desirable to "pass," but that option doesn't exist in chess!

Take a look at this materially even pawn endgame. It's white's move.

White to move and win

1. b8(Q)+! Kxb8 2. a6

This is the *Zugzwang* position! Black has only two options, both of them bad. He can choose to move his king from the only position that holds off the two white pawns from queening. Or he can move his own pawns from the only position that prevents white's king from gobbling them up! Let's look at the first option:

2. ... Kc7

2. ... Ka7 comes to the same end.

3. a7

And the a-pawn queens by marching straight ahead. Now let's look at black's other choice, moving a pawn. Keep in mind the important concept of *Zugzwang*. Picking the game up after 2. a6:

2. ... h3+ 3. Kxh3

Black is again in Zugzwang!

Now another pawn move loses the remaining two pawns. And we've just seen what moving the king allows. Black, a victim of *Zugzwang*, is lost.

Go back to the very first diagram. Note that if white plays 1. a6??, black slides his king back to b8, stymieing white's pawn advance, and turning the tables! White would then wish *he* could pass! He would have to move his king from the only square that can prevent black's pawns from advancing: 1. ... Kb8 2. Kh3 (moving the king backward also loses) f3 3. a7+ Kxa7 4. b8Q+ Kxb8 5. c7+ Kxc7, and, finally, white would have to move his king to the fourth rank, allowing black to queen.

Sacrifice for a common goal: the pawn breakthrough

With the kings distant and only the black pawns to stand in the way of the more advanced white pawns, can white force one through to promotion and win the game? If it's his move, he can. This is definitely a pawn trick worth knowing!

**White to move and win—
without moving his king!**

1. b6! cxb6

If ... axb6 2. c6 bxc6 3. a6.

2. a6

White's technique becomes clear. Whatever black does, one of white's pawns will queen.

2. ... bxa6

Or 2. ... bxc5 3. axb7.

3. c6

This three-pawn breakthrough technique works only if no other pieces can interfere with the battle of the pawns. Here, for instance, black's king is too far away, by two tempos, to catch the c-pawn. Try this trick out in various circumstances to see what works and what doesn't—and what happens when the defending pawns are farther advanced.

In the original diagram, if black has the move, he can stop white's intention with 1. ... b6! leading to a draw: 2. axb6 axb6 3. c6! (3. cxb6 also draws, but from a position of weakness)

3. ... Kg5 4. Kg3 Kf5 5. Kf3 Ke5 6. Kg4 Ke4 7. Kg5 Ke5 (the attempt to win with 7. ... Kd5 loses, as white's c-pawn queens much earlier than black's b-pawn) 8. Kg6 Ke6 9. Kg5 Ke5, etc.

Play over the examples in this section from time to time. Remember that the point is to get a feel for how the various pieces can work together—in sometimes surprising ways!

Level II, Lesson Four
Memory Markers!

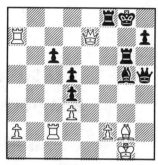

White to move   **White to move**

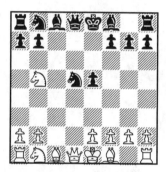

Black to move   **White to move**

Solutions:

MM1: **1. ... Qxe3 2. fxe3** (or 2. Bf4 Rxf2!, with the same outcome) **2. ... Rg2+ 3. Kh1 Rxh2+ 4. Kg1 Rcg2#.** Note how white's f1-rook blocks the white king's escape.

MM2: **1. Bxd5+ cxd5 2. Qxf8+ Kxf8 3. Rc8+,** and mate next move.

MM3: **1. Qxd5! Qxd5 2. Nc7+.** White wins a knight. A common trick!

MM4: 1. Qxe6+, winning. If 1. ... fxe6, 2. Bg6#, with a crisscrossing mate (Alekhine—Vasic, 1931).

**"Tactics flow from
a superior position."
—Bobby Fischer**

—Level II—

Lesson Five

Tools of the Trade

*In this lesson, you will learn to use the most effective chess
tactics to win material or even checkmate.*

I f the number of wins per page could be calculated, we'd bet that this chapter would be the top scorer. It teaches you the fundamental tactics that can be used to win material, and you've already seen how being ahead in material can be converted to a win.

It helps to distinguish between tactics and strategy by explaining that tactics are the short-term cut and thrust of chess and that strategy, which you'll study later, is the long-term planning of the game. The more you know about chess, the more you see that this distinction often becomes blurred, but it's still a useful definition to begin with.

In Lesson Two, in order to be able to beat most of the chess players you'll encounter, you learned just the three most common tactics—*double attack, skewer, and pin.* In Lesson Four, you saw two more—*discovered attack,* in the form of the discovered check used in the "Windmill" example, and a *double check* you saw in smothered mate. But to compete against

On a wins-per-page scale, this chapter may be the top scorer!

tournament players, you need to know more.

Before introducing new tactics, let's quickly review the five you've already seen. Note that over time, chess players have given names to the most frequently occurring tactical ideas. Knowing their names gives you an easy way to talk and think about them. But, as always, remembering the ideas is the most important takeaway.

Tactic #1: double attack

As you've seen, a double attack is a single move that makes two separate threats at the same time. Let's see how the double attack can be applied in a realistic game position.

Botvinnik—Golombek
1956

White to move

Botvinnik plays a combination—a forced sequence of moves that will change the balance of the game. This one will end in a winning double attack:

1. Bxg7! Kxg7 (Black's king has been moved to a vulnerable square.) **2. Rc1 Qd7 3. a4! Nc7 4. Qc3+**, attacking both the king and *adding* an attacker against the knight.

White's 4. Qc3+ is a double attack.

In this example, by the way, if black had tried 3. ... Na3, 4. Qb2+! again wins the knight with a double attack.

Obviously, when two of your enemy's men are attacked, he finds it very difficult to save both of them!

Tactic #2: skewer

The shish kebab of chess, a skewer attacks the more valuable of two pieces along a diagonal, rank or file, forcing it to move and expose the less valuable piece behind it to capture.

**Brundtrup—Burdick
1954**

White to move and win.

White to move and pin.

In the position above, white sets up a winning skewer using the decoy technique you'll learn in this lesson. We'll preview it to you now: **1. Qg1+!**. (You can see that this move is both a *double attack* and a *sacrifice*. The chess ideas you learn overlap and build on one another.) With this move, white *decoys* black's queen to g1. **1. ... Qxg1**. Now white plays the skewering move: **2. g8(Q)+**. White spears the black queen through her king, and winds up a full queen ahead.

Tactic #3: pin

The pin is the flip side of the skewer. Your pin attacks one of two enemy pieces along the same diagonal, rank or file. The enemy piece in front can't move without exposing the piece behind it, normally the more valuable man.

This position features pins and counter-pins. Can you predict white's next move?

1. Bc5! (pinning the black queen to her king!) **1. ... Bb6!** (the only defense here, pinning the white bishop to its king, but ...) **2. Qf4+!!** (double-attacking the king and pinned queen, winning.)

Tactic #4: discovered attack

By employing a discovered attack, you move one piece, exposing an attack from a different piece lurking behind it. That can be a very unpleasant surprise for the defender!

White plays 1. Ng5, attacking black's rook on h7 while discovering an attack by the white bishop on the other rook on a8.

A discovered attack often amounts to a free move for the attacker. A very powerful form of the discovered attack is the *discovered check*. (You saw an example of discovered check in the "Windmill" in Lesson Four.) The attacker's hidden piece threatens the enemy king. The defender has no choice but to get out of the check, while often not being able to defend against other, simultaneous threats delivered by the other piece.

Short—Ludgate
1977

White to move.

Here a discovered check unleashes the power of the passed pawn:

1. Qg7+! Qxg7 2. e7+!!, winning.

This next example isn't a discovered check, it's a simple example of a discovered attack with check—that is, the discovering piece gives the check. The discovered attack has quite a powerful effect in this form as well.

White plays 1. Be5+, attacking black's king on h8 while discovering an attack by the white rook on the black rook on d8.

Discovered attacks, especially discovered checks, can be devastating.

Tactic #5: double check

Double check is the nuclear warhead of chess. It's sort of discovered attack on steroids—one of your pieces moves, giving check, and at the same time uncovers another of your pieces that gives check as well. Obviously, your opponent can't capture or block both attackers at once, so the enemy king's defense is limited to moving. And if he can't move, it's checkmate!

1. Bb5++!!, checkmate!

In this example, after **1. Bb5++!!** ("++" indicates double check), even though white's bishop on b5 is attacked, it can't be taken because the white rook on e1 is also putting black's king in check. And since black's king can't move out of check, it's mate.

Tactic #6: decoy

The decoy diverts an enemy piece *to* a certain square. In the diagram below, white decoys black's queen to c7 so white can win the lady with 2. Qh7+.

White plays 1. Rc7!

White forces the black queen to capture the rook on c7, moving farther away from her king. Then 2. Qh7+ skewers the black queen.

Two important subjects: combination and sacrifice

There are two terms that you will run across again and again in your study of chess—*combination* and *sacrifice*. Chess players call a series of moves that force a change in the position to one side's advantage a *combination*. A combination frequently starts with a *sacrifice*—a move that voluntarily gives up material for some kind of resulting greater gain.

In the example of decoy at left, below, you can see that it is actually a blend of two simpler tactics you've already learned. It starts with the sacrifice of the rook to force the queen to c7 by pinning the queen to the king— the queen must take the rook or be captured. Once the enemy queen has been forced to the decoy square of c7, 2. Qh7+ then skewers the queen. (Note that the immediate 1. Qh7+ is simply met with 1. ... Ke6, defending the queen.)

Tactic #7: deflection

Deflection diverts an enemy man *from* a particular square. (Decoy = *to* a square; deflection = *from* a square.)

White plays 1. Rg5!, forcing 1. ... Rxg5, allowing the white pawn to queen!

In the following example, black twice uses *deflection* to win the enemy knight. Note the *motifs* that should have alerted you to search hard for a winning blow: white's weak back rank, and the undefended knight.

Black plays 1. ... Qd5, to deflect white's queen from her army's back rank.

1. ... Qd5! **2. Qc1** (White's queen can't capture on d5 because of 2. ... Re1#—a back-rank motif.) **2. ... Qxg5.**

Note that black's last move highlights yet another motif,

overloading. (See Tactic #12, page 84.) White's queen can't guard both the knight and the back rank.

♛♛♛♛♛

Before moving on, we can't resist showing you this beautiful example of diversion by José Raúl Capablanca, one of your authors' chess heroes.

Bernstein—Capablanca
1914

Black to move and win with a deflection combination.

1. ... Qb2! (in the actual game, white resigned here) **2. Rc8!?** (2. Rc2 Qb1+ 3. Qf1 Qxc2; or 2. Qe1 Qxc3 3. Qxc3 Rd1+ 4. Qe1 Rxe1#) **2. ... Qb1+** (an *in-between move*—see tactic 11) **3. Qf1 Qxf1+** (one more *in-between* move) **4. Kxf1 Rxc8** **0-1**.

Tactic #8: back-rank mate

Back-rank mates, like that in the diagram above, occur frequently. A king, hemmed in by his own pawns, is checkmated on his back rank. The final, sad result leaves a situation like this:

Black is checkmated on the back rank, despite his material superiority.

Strictly speaking, the back-rank mate is a theme based on a weakness on a player's first rank, rather than a tactic. But it is so frequently a game-winner or at least a compelling threat, that it makes sense to list it here. Often, but not always, the way to exploit an opponent's weak back rank is to use *deflection*.

♛♛♛♛♛

Take a close look at the following position. Can you apply the theme of back-rank mate to find the winning move for black?

Black to move and win.

1. ... Rd8!

White must exchange his queen for the black rook, because if she moves off the d-file (i.e., 2. Qxe7), 2. ... Rxd1 delivers the back-rank mate. Actually, this is an easy move to find if you know the theme, although some would suffer a mental block to giving up the black queen. But respect for the queen's value shouldn't be an obsession. Remember, the queen is worth nine points, but the value of the king is infinite!

Tactic #9: blocking

Blocking limits the mobility of an enemy piece in some critical way. This tactic is often used against the opponent's king to deliver checkmate.

White plays 1. Ra3+!
after the forced 1. ... Bxa3, 2. b3!#

In the beautiful example above, white sacrifices his last piece, forcing black to block the a3 square, thus allowing white to checkmate with his last pawn!

Tactic #10: interference

This tactic is defined clearly from its name:

Nenarokov—Grigoriev
1923

Black to move.

In this endgame, black has two pawns moving toward the goal of promotion. The white rook restrains black's pawn on d2, while white's bishop must stop black's h-pawn from advancing. Do you see a move for black that interferes with white's defenses?

1. ... Bd6!!. Wonderful—double interference! Either the d-file or the h2-b8 diagonal will be blocked, and black will queen one of his passed pawns and win.

Tactic #11: in-between move

The in-between move is the mother of all surprise moves. You'll sometimes see the German word for it— *Zwischenzug* (pronounced TSVISH-en-tsoogk). Your opponent makes a move that he thinks forces a certain reply, but you come up with a different move that turns the tables. Ah, *Schadenfreude*!

In the diagram below, white's king has attacked black's knight, and black has answered by moving his bishop to counter-attack white's knight. But that *Zwischenzug* was a serious error. White has a new in-between move that wins.

After 1. Kd3 Ba5

2. b4!, and wins—if 2. ... Bxb4, 3. Nc2, turning the counterattack back onto black and winning a piece with a double attack.

Tactic #12: overloading

Overloading is really a theme, like back-rank mate. When a piece has too many duties, it's a weak point in the enemy camp. You may be able to apply one of the basic tactics to take advantage of its plight. Look at the simplified example at the top of the next column. It's white's move. Black's bishop on d6 is tasked with preventing checkmate on both b8 and f8. It's overloaded, and we can apply the tactic of deflection.

1. Rb8+! Bxb8 2. Rf8#

Now let's examine a more complicated example.

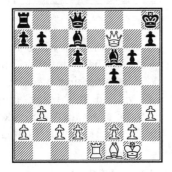

White to move

Notice that black's queen defends both black's light- and dark-squared bishops, and the latter is the key defender of its king. White finds a winning move that combines a number of ideas that we've studied.

1. Re8+! (black can't play 1. … Bxe8? because there's a show-closing interference theme— 2. Qf8#) **1. … Qxe8 2. Qxf6+ Kg8 3. Bc4+**, and wins.

Tactic #13: clearance

A clearance move (sometimes it's a clearance sacrifice) vacates a critical square to open a line or square.

**Benko—Fuester
1958**

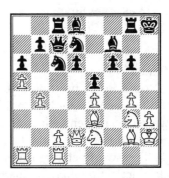

White to move

1. Bb6!.

This clearance move uses the tactic of double attack—with the bishop removed from e3, white threatens 2. Qh6 mate, while the bishop on b6 threatens the black queen. Black resigns. How do you find such a blow? Try a little daydreaming sometimes—"If not for that bishop, I'd mate him in one …"

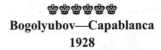

**Bogolyubov—Capablanca
1928**

Black to mate in two.

Here a *clearance sacrifice* allows black to mate in two!

1. ... Nc5+!. White can't avoid **2. ... e4#**.

Tactic #14: eliminating the defender

Notice in the position below that only one of white's men, his pawn on f2, prevents black from checkmating white with **1. ... Qg3**. Then-world-champ Karpov finds a deflection that eliminates this key defender.

Tarjan—Karpov
1976

1. ... Re3+!

Sometimes eliminating the defender takes the form of destroying the pawn cover in front of the enemy king. Study how three-time U.S. Champion Gata Kamsky brilliantly uses this idea to defeat French champion Joel Lautier.

Kamsky—Lautier
Dortmund, 1993

At the moment, white does not seem to have much of an attack. The attacking pieces are far away, and the black king seems to be adequately defended by the wall of pawns. Things change quickly!

1. Bxh6! gxh6 2. Qxh6

By giving away a bishop for two pawns, white has managed to destroy the pawn cover of the enemy king and create serious threats to black's monarch. Two pawns are not full compensation for a piece, but together with attacking chances they can be enough or more, especially if white can bring in other forces.

By exposing the black king, white creates new motifs for threats and combinations. White's main problem now is how to get a decisive concentration of force against the enemy king.

2. ... Re8

This invites white to win the black queen by playing Bh7+ with a discovered attack on the d-file, but that would not be good for white, who has already sacrificed a bishop. After all, rook and bishop are almost equal to the queen, and rook and two bishops will be stronger here than a queen and two pawns.

3. Bc4!

Black's last move does make some breathing space for the king, but it also has the drawback of weakening the f7-square. White's brilliant move not only takes control of the a2-g8 diagonal but also allows the white queen to make use of the g6-square since the pawn at f7 is now pinned. In addition, the line between the rook at d1 and queen at d8 is now open, and the rook can also transfer to the kingside via d4 or d3.

3. ... Bd7

Black tries to control some light squares, but this doesn't help.

4. Rd4 Bf8 5. Qg6+ Bg7
6. Qxf7+ Kh8 7. Rh4+ Nh7
8. Rxh7+!

8. ... Kxh7 9. Qh5+ Bh6
10. Bd3+ Kg8 11. Qxh6

Black gives up. Not only do white's three pawns more than compensate for the Exchange (knight-for-rook), but black's king is hopelessly exposed.

Tactic #15: desperado

Desperado is another theme. Think of it as the kamikaze chess piece. It's often used to draw by stalemate.

Black to move

1. Rh7+ Kg3 2. Rf7—for example, 2. ... Rg8 3. Rg7, continuing to shadow the black rook along the seventh rank. Capturing white's rook produces instant stalemate.

As we've seen, several tactical ideas can be combined into one idea or, on the other hand, divided into parts. And there are other tactical themes, ideas, and motifs we will learn later.

Level II, Lesson Five
Memory Markers!

After 1. ... Re8

MEMORY MARKER 1

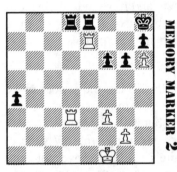

White to move

MEMORY MARKER 2

Black to move

MEMORY MARKER 3

White to move

MEMORY MARKER 4

Solutions:

MM1: Black's last move was 1. ... Rf8-e8, perhaps hoping for 2. Rxe8+ Qxe8, and black is up an Exchange. (Black should have returned the Exchange with 1. ... Qd7). White now ignores black's threat to take his e1-rook (with a check!) and creates his own superior, unstoppable threat—a sort of *Zwischenzug*. **2. Qf7 Rxe1+ 3. Kh2**, and there is no defense against mating threats (e.g., 3. ... Qg8, 4. Qxf6+).

MM2: **1. Rdd7**, with checkmate in four moves or less.

MM3: **1. ... Rb8 2. Ba4 Kf7 3. e8=Q+**, with a drawish ending. But first you should have found that the natural (and ambitious) 1. ... Kf7 loses to 2. e8=Q+ (decoy!) 2. ... Kxe8 3. Ba4 (pin and win!).

MM4: **1. Qg3! Qxh6+** (1. ... Rxg3 2. Rxe8(++) checkmate) **2. Qh3 Qd6 3. Kh1**

After 3. Kh1

3. ... Kg8 (there's no other defense here) **4. Rxe8+ Kf7 5. Rh8**, winning (Duras—Spielmann, 1912).

"Beware of Greeks bearing gifts."
—Virgil

—Level II—

Lesson Six

Bishop Sacrifices

In this lesson, you'll learn two important bishop-sacrifice patterns, and you'll learn a lot about when a sacrificial attack works and when it doesn't.

The very possibility of a sacrifice makes a chess heart beat faster. Let's take a look at two famous types of bishop sacrifices. Analyzing these examples can teach you a lot about attack and defense and how to evaluate the correctness of a sacrifice.

The most important sacrifice—*"Beware of Greeks bearing gifts!"*

There's an important sacrificial theme against the castled king that occurs so often that chess players have a name for it—the *Greek Gift*. Perhaps it's named after the famous story of the Greeks who left a huge wooden horse as an apparent gift for the defenders of the ancient city of Troy, who took it inside their walls. But when night came, the Greek warriors hidden inside of the horse crept out and opened the gates for the rest of their army, capturing the city and its king.

In chess, however, the Greek Gift normally starts with the gift of a bishop, not a horse—and it's important to note that the defend-

The Greek Gift sacrifice is the most important sacrifice in chess!

er doesn't usually have a choice as to whether to accept the gift. The square on which the bishop sacrifices itself is h7.

After **1. Bxh7+ Kxh7 2. Ng5+ Kg8 3. Qh5 Bxg5 4. hxg5** (opening up the h-file, unmasking the white rook's power) **4. ... f5** (Black tries to create a flight square) **5. g6** (White slams the door shut; checkmate is now unstoppable).

After 2. Nxg5

If black tries 2. ... Bxg5, then 3. hxg5+ Kg6 4. Qh5+ Kf5 5. g6+, leading to mate.

Or, if 2. ... Kg6, then 3. h5+ Kh6 4. Nxf7++ wins the queen.

White's main agents in this lightning-attack were the light-square bishop on d3, the queen on d1, the knight on f3, which leaps to g5 with check—and the dark-square bishop which supports the action from its starting position on c1. Note that white's e5-pawn prevented black from defending against 4. Qh7# with 3. ... Nf6. And since the black bishop on e7 guards the g5-square, the combination succeeded only because of the pawn at h4, backed up by the rook at h1.

Play over these lines on your own board, beginning with the diagram at top left. If you can find moves for black that leave him with a better or even equal position, white's sacrifice is incorrect. Even though we're sure the sequence above wins for white, your trying hard to refute the sacrifice will build your attack and defense muscles. (And, as a chess player, you should believe only what you can prove to yourself. Sometimes the books are wrong!)

Don't get the impression that Bxh7+ checkmates every time! Let's look at another example.

Don't get the impression that Bxh7+ wins every time.

**1. e4 e6 2. d4 d5 3. Nc3 Nf6
4. e5 Nfd7 5. Nf3 c5 6.dxc5
Bxc5 7. Bd3 0–0**

11. Qxf7+ Kh8 12. Qh5+ Kg8
13. Qh7+ Kf8 14. Qh8+

14. … Ke7 15. Qxg7#

10. Qd3+ f5

8. Bxh7+! Kxh7 (Otherwise,
black is simply down a pawn and
his king is wide open to attack.)
9. Ng5+

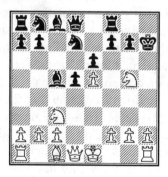

9. … Kg6

If 9. … Kg8? 10. Qh5 Re8

11. Qg3

White has some advantage in
a complex position. (The tempt-
ing move 11. Nxe6 is not good
here because of 11. ... Bxf2+, and
if 12. Kxf2? Qb6+, a double
attack.) In general, positions
after Ng5+, in which black plays
... Kg8, can be calculated to their
conclusions to be in either
white's or black's favor. But
when black responds with ...
Kg6, the positions are often
unclear.

Here's another example that draws some subtle contrasts with the previous one.

1. e4 e6 2. d4 d5 3. Nc3 Bb4 4. e5 Ne7 5. Bd3 0–0 6. Nf3 c5? (Relatively best was 6. ... h6.)

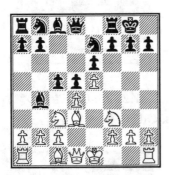

7. Bxh7+ Kxh7 8. Ng5+ Kg8 (or 8. ... Kg6 9. h4!, with the threat of 10. h5+!) **9. Qh5 Re8**

(forced—to give the black king a flight square) **10. Qh7+** (not 10. Qxf7+, as played in a previous example; in a few moves, you'll see why) **10. ... Kf8 11. Qh8+**

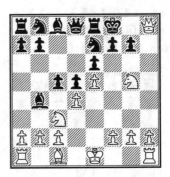

11. ... Ng8 12. Nh7+ Ke7 (with the f7-pawn gone—see note to 10. Qh7+—black could play ... Kf7 and hold) **13. Bg5+,** winning.

Although there are whole books written just on the subject of when this sacrifice works and when it doesn't, our few examples above give you a good foundation of understanding for this frequent theme in the attack against the castled king. In the cat-and-mouse game of chess, expert defenders sometimes even tease the attacker into trying the sacrifice when it is not good! Play over the games in this short chapter until you feel you've mastered their ideas.

The two-bishop sacrifice— doubling down on the Greek Gift

Let's look at another sacrificial theme against the castled king that in poker terms "doubles down" on the last section. When, in 1889, Emanuel Lasker played this idea successfully for the first time, it made headlines all over the world. In our own time, the great world champion Garry Kasparov quipped that, had Lasker played it today, he would have applied for a patent! Once again, you can learn a lot about kingside attacks by carefully studying this idea.

Lasker—Bauer
Amsterdam, 1889

1. f4 d5 2. e3 Nf6 3. b3 e6 4. Bb2 Be7 5. Bd3 b6 6. Nf3 Bb7 7. Nc3 Nbd7 8. 0–0 0–0 9. Ne2 c5 10. Ng3 Qc7 11. Ne5 Nxe5 12. Bxe5 Qc6 13. Qe2 a6 14. Nh5 Nxh5

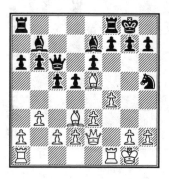

Black has just played 14. ... Nf6xh5, putting himself temporarily a piece up.

However, white's two bishops sit on the long diagonals a1-h8 and b1-h7; black's king has inadequate protection; and white's queen and a rook are in position to support the attack.

Lasker, playing in his *first* major tournament, uncorks the pioneering double-bishop sac:

15. Bxh7+! Kxh7 16. Qxh5+ Kg8

17. Bxg7! Kxg7

Rejecting the offer of the second bishop-gift doesn't save black here, e.g.: 17. ... f5 18. Be5, or 17. ... f6 18. Bh6, with deadly threats in both cases.

18. Qg4+ Kh7 19. Rf3.

This attacking maneuver is logically called a "rook lift," since the major piece is being "lifted" into the fray. The threat is now 20. Rh3#. Black must hurry to be able to block, even though it requires giving up his queen.

Lasker's last move double-attacks the two enemy bishops, winning material—a wonderfully wry twist to the first successful two-bishop sacrifice on record!

Lasker's game produced a great impression on his contemporaries, but nowadays this sort of sacrifice has become rather routine at master levels.

**19. ... e5 20. Rh3+ Qh6
21. Rxh6+ Kxh6 22. Qd7!**

Level II, Lesson Six
Memory Markers!

MEMORY MARKER 1

Black to move

MEMORY MARKER 2

White to move

MEMORY MARKER 3

White to move

MEMORY MARKER 4

White to move

Solutions:

MM1: **1. ... Kg8!** (not 1. ... Kg6 2. Qe4+ f5 3. exf6 ep+ Kxf6 4. Qxe6#)
2. Qh5 N5f6 3. exf6 Nxf6 4. Qh4 e5±. (Valickova—Stodolova, 2001)

MM2: **1. Qg4!** (1. Qd3+ Nf5 leads to approximate equality **1. ... Nxe5**
2. Rxe5 f5 3. Qh4 Bc8. White won now after 4. Nxe6; perhaps even more
forceful was 4. Qh7+, according to Rybka. (Carlsen—Martinez, 2008)

MM3: **1. Nc6! Bxc6 2. Bxh7+! Kxh7 3. Qh5+ Kg8 4. Bxg7! Kxg7**
5. Rg3+ Kf6 6. Re1!.

MM4: **1. Bxh7+ Kxh7 2. Rh3+ Kg8 3. Bxg7!**, and black resigned. In
this position the best move is 3. ...f6, but then 4. Bh6! Qh7 5. Qh5! Bf8
(or 5. ... Be8 6. Rg3+ Kh8 7. Bg7+ and 8. Bxf6+) 6. Qg4+ Kh8 7. Bxf8.
(Alekhine—Drewitt, 1923)

"Conduct the attack so that when the fire is out ... it isn't."

—Reuben Fine

—Level II—

Lesson Seven

Attacking the King

In this lesson, you'll learn techniques for attacking and defending the king, whether it's castled or not.

The attacks against the king can be usefully divided into three circumstances—when the defender's king is still in the center, when both players have castled kingside, and when the players have castled on opposite sides. (Games in which both players have castled queenside are very rare.) We'll take a look at all three of these situations in this chapter.

Attack against the uncastled king

We've already seen a number of examples illustrating the dangers to the uncastled king. For the sake of completeness in this chapter, we'll look at a few more.

1. d4 Nf6 2. Nd2 e5 3. dxe5 Ng4 4. h3? Ne3

Since white's queen is smothered, he must capture the enemy knight.

5. fxe3 Qh4+ 6. g3 Qxg3#

In the 1. e4 e5 openings, the f7-square is the most vulnerable before castling (not so often f2, as white has an extra tempo, and thus—more often—the initiative.).

1. e4 e5 2. Nf3 d6 3. d4 Nd7 4. Bc4!

Now 4. … Be7? (to stop 5. Ng5) is met by 5. dxe5 dxe5 6. Qd5

Black can't effectively defend against the threat of mate on f7. If 6. … Nh6, 7. Bxh6, and the mate threat is on again. White ends up a piece ahead.

If 4. … Ngf6, then 5. dxe5

5. … Nxe5 (5. … dxe5, then 6. Ng5; and if 5. … Nxe4 6. Qd5) 6. Nxe5 dxe5 7. Bxf7+

White wins a pawn after 7. … Ke7. If 7. … Kxf7, then 8. Qxd8 Bb4+ 9. Qd2

9. … Bxd2+ 10. Nxd2. ♚♚♚♚♚♚

Preventing, or even delaying, castling by your opponent is worth sacrificing a pawn.

Here's an early attack in the Caro-Kann Defense. (We'll study openings and their names later.)

1. e4 c6 2. d4 d5 3. Nc3 dxe4 4. Nxe4 Nd7 5. Bc4 Ngf6 6. Ng5 e6 7. Qe2

White is poised to play a devastating 8. Nxf7!: for example, 7. ... Be7 8. Nxf7 Kxf7 9. Qxe6+ Kg6 10. Bd3+ Kh5 11. Qh3#, or 7. ... h6 8. Nxf7, with the same outcome.

So black must play 7. ... Nb6 or 7. ... Nd5, with an approximately equal game.

Attack against the castled king—with pieces

A castled king is much safer than a king in the center—that's why you want to castle quickly!

In most tournament games, the players castle kingside, because, after all, this can normally be accomplished in fewer moves than queenside castling. Sometimes an attack against the castled king can be conducted entirely with pieces.

**Alekhine–Sterk
Budapest, 1921**

After 22. .... Na4

Since black's pieces are tied up on the queenside, Alekhine, a future world champion, starts an attack on the opposite side of the board. (White cannot win a piece with 23. b4 because of the reply 23. ... Nc3; white must also watch out for black's threat of 23. ... Rac8, exploiting the pin on his rook.)

23. Bf6 (white's bishop is

Drawing your opponent's king into the real center of the board is generally worth the sacrifice of a piece!

immune—if 23. ... gxf6, 24. Rg4+ wins the queen—a pin becomes a double attack!) **23. ... Rfc8 24. Qe5**

Black must defend against 25. Qg5, as well as 25. Rg4, and so he cannot capture either the rook or the bishop (for example—24. ... gxf6 25. Rg4+ Kf8 26. Qd6+ and 27. Rg8#).

24. ... Rc5 25. Qg3

White wins a knight—and with it, the game: **25. ... g6 26. Rxa4**, and black resigned in a few moves.

♛♛♛♛♛

Let's look at a game that shows us the third world champion, José Capablanca, attacking with pieces against the castled king.

Capablanca–Levenfish
Moscow, 1935

Once the white queen and bishop are lined up against h7, black's knight on f6 is the only piece holding black's game together. Now, to avoid mate, black must weaken his kingside with either ... g6 or ... h6. But in this position, either move leads to a telling loss of material.

19. ... h6

Or 19. ... g6 20. Nc6 Qd5 21. Bxf6 Qxc6 22. Qh6, followed by 23. Qg7#.

20. Ng4!

Also possible is 20. Bxh6, but Capablanca's move is stronger.

20. .. Be7

Here Capablanca played **21. Bxf6** and won. But he missed a forced mate using a pattern we've studied!

21. Nxh6+ gxh6 22. Bxf6 Bxf6 23. Qxh6 Re8 24. Bh7+ Kh8 25. Bg6+ Kg8 26. Qh7+ Kf8 27. Qxf7# Damiano's mate!

Attack against the same-side castled king—with pawns

Sometimes the attacker launches a *pawn storm* by moving the pawns in front of his own king. This kind of attack can be very committal—if it doesn't pan out, the attacker might become the defender!

Let's look at a game played by the very first official world champion, Wilhelm Steinitz, almost 150 years ago.

1. e4 e5 2. Nf3 d6 3. Bc4 Be7 4. c3 Nf6 5. d3 0–0 6. 0–0 Bg4 7. h3 Bxf3 8. Qxf3 c6 9. Bb3 Nbd7 10. Qe2 Nc5 11. Bc2 Ne6 12. g3 Qc7 13. f4

**Steinitz–MacDonnell
Dublin, 1865**

13. ... Rfe8

Taking on f4 was a lesser evil, because after 14. f4-f5 (played on move 16), white is strategically won. (But in 1865, this idea was not well known yet—and that fact explains the next few moves for both sides.)

14. Nd2 Rad8 15. Nf3 Kh8 16. f5 (at last!) **16. ... Nf8 17. g4**

17. ... h6 18. g5 (opening the g-file for a coming assault) **18. ... hxg5 19. Nxg5 Kg8 20. Kh1 N6h7 21. Nf3**

White has more space and the attack: two valid reasons to reject the trade.

21. ... Rd7 22. Rg1 Bd8 23. Bh6 f6 24. Rg2 d5

25. Rag1 Ree7 26. exd5 cxd5 27. Ba4 (winning material) **27. ... Rd6 28. Rxg7+ Rxg7 29. Rxg7+ Qxg7 30. Bxg7**

White, materially ahead, went on to win.

Attack when kings are castled on opposite sides

When the opponents castle on opposite sides of the board, normally the first player to get an effective attack going wins, and normally these attacks involve pawn storms, since in these cases, pushing pawns against your opponent does not destroy the shelter in front of your own king. Let's look at a famous game by Boris Spassky, who went on to become the 10th world champion.

1. d4 Nf6 2. c4 g6 3. Nc3 Bg7 4. e4 d6 5. f3 c6 6. Be3 a6

Spassky–Evans
Varna, 1962

White intends to attack on the kingside, where black must castle sooner or later. Black prepares operations on the other side of the board.

7. Qd2 b5 8. 0–0–0 bxc4 (other options were 8. ... Qa5 or 8. ... 0-0) **9. Bxc4 0–0 10. h4**

The pawn storm begins.

10. ... d5

Countering a flank attack with a central counter-thrust is a natural and logical plan. But right now it may be better to play 10. ... h5 and slow down the pawn storm, even though it weakens the kingside slightly.

11. Bb3 dxe4

Now it's too late for 11. ... h5 because of 12. e5 Ne8 13. g4 hxg4 14. h5, when the opening of the h-file will be fatal for black because of the absence of a knight on f6.

12. h5!

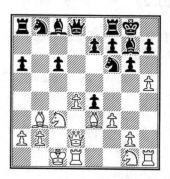

12. ... exf3

Bad for black is 12. ... Nxh5 13. g4 Nf6 14. Bh6 (or 14. Qh2

fxe4 15. Nxe4 Nbd7 16. g5 Nh5 17. Ng3). White need not be concerned about losing kingside pawns, since their absence only opens lines and helps his attack.

13. hxg6 hxg6 14. Bh6! fxg2 15. Rh4

This position confirms the correctness of white's plan: The h-file is open and available for use by white's heavy artillery. The next stage for white is to exchange the dark-square defender at g7 to further weaken black's kingside. Black cannot block the h-file with 15. ... Nh5 because the simple 16. Rxh5 gxh5 17. Qg5 forces checkmate.

15. ... Ng4 16. Bxg7 Kxg7 17. Qxg2

The threat is 18. Rxg4. Note that 17. ... Ne3? is not possible because of 18. Qh2 Rh8 19. Rxh8 Qxh8 20. Qe5+, winning the knight on e3. If 17. ... f5, 18. Nf3 Rh8 19. Rdh1 Rxh4 20. Rxh4 Nd7 21. Rh7+!

Note the weakness of the light squares near the black king. Wherever the black king moves, he's caught in a king-queen fork.

17. ... Nh6

Black's best was 17. ... Rh8, conceding white a significant advantage after 18. Rxg4—according to the computer program Rybka.

18. Nf3 Nf5 19. Rh2 Qd6

If 19. ... Ne3, then 20. Qh1! is conclusive—for example, 20. ... Rh8 21. Ng5 Rxh2 22. Qxh2 (Rybka), when white's attack is unstoppable. 20. Qg5 also wins. And 19. ... Rh8 loses to 20. Bxf7.

20. Ne5 Nd7 21. Ne4 Qc7 22. Rdh1

White completely dominates the h-file, and all of his pieces are very active. White's attacking plan has succeeded, and the end is near.

22. ... Rg8 (if 22. ... Nf6, then 23. Bxf7! or 23. Nxf6! force checkmate) **23. Rh7+ Kf8 24. Rxf7+ Ke8 25. Qxg6 Nxe5 26. Rf8++**

It's mate next move. This game brilliantly demonstrates how to open and use the rook file to attack an opponent castled on the opposite side of the board.

Level II, Lesson Seven
Memory Markers!

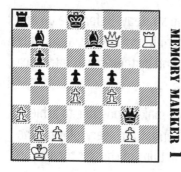

Black to move

MEMORY MARKER 1

White to move

MEMORY MARKER 2

White to move

MEMORY MARKER 3

Black to move

MEMORY MARKER 4

Solutions:

MM1: **1. ... Qe1+ 2. Ka2 Qb4,** winning. If 3. Rh8+ Kd7 4. Rxa8, then 4. ... Qc4+: An example of the side with his king in the center refuting the attack.

MM2: **1. f5!** with advantage for white. (Reti—Carls, 1925)

MM3: **1. Qh5 h6 2. Rxe6 fxe6 3. Qg6,** winning. (Ciocaltea—Sandor, 1969)

MM4: Botvinnik once called a chess game a sequence of trade-offs—not just of pieces and pawns, but also of various strengths and weaknesses. Here we have a typical castled-on-opposite-sides-and-attacks-are-coming position. So far. **1. ... c4!.** This move gives white firm control of the d4 square. Why? **2. Be2 a6!!** Remember this technique! Now a5 is met by ... b5, and b5 is met by ... a5, keeping the queenside closed while black's kingside attack will roll on. (Spassky—Petrosian, 1966)

Introduction to Strategy

The next series of chapters will take up strategy. Before we go any farther, let's define a few terms. These definitions are not absolutely rigid—but they're useful generalizations, and by themselves introduce important strategic concepts.

A *plan* is a visualized series of steps that make it possible to achieve a goal. Learning to plan is absolutely essential for every player who wishes to improve. Indeed, one of the attractions of chess is the way in which it teaches foresight and planning.

Strategy is the art of forming an overall plan. Strategy is the "grand scheme" for a game. In a sense, strategy is the opposite of tactics, which are the application of a short series of forced moves to achieve an immediate improvement. The words *positional* and *strategic* are frequently used interchangeably.

It's very important to understand that the correct strategic planning *dictates* the choice of objectives. The significance of this idea is often understated. A player must evaluate the position on the board before him in order to come up with a plan. For example, he should not decide to attack the opponent's king unless the position calls for it.

This book will take the mystery out of positional analysis. We're fortunate to have the benefit of the great masters, notably the first world champion, Wilhelm Steinitz, to show us how to evaluate positions logically and methodically.

Wilhem Steinitz, the first official world champion, was the "godfather" of modern strategy.

Steinitz shows us that there are four logical steps—that must be followed in order—to find an appropriate strategy in any position.

1. Divide the position into *elements* (see below)
2. Evaluate the position by comparing the elements of white's and black's positions
3. Determine a plan
4. Look for a specific move

We'll examine a number of positional elements:

1. Development
2. Activity (sometimes called mobility)
3. The center
4. The positions of the kings
5. Weak and strong squares in both camps
6. Pawn structures
7. Open files
8. Two bishops against bishop and knight or against two knights

These elements are interconnected (indeed, interchangeable): control of the center and activity of the pieces depend on pawn structure, while active pieces may negate structural weaknesses. (Without rooks and queens, for example, what special good are open files?)

Based on these elements, a chess player can evaluate a position and develop a strategic plan. The evaluation includes assessing who is better and by how much, or whether the position is equal. But evaluation goes beyond this to enumerate specific strengths and weaknesses of both armies. The evaluation must be confirmed by concrete, move-by-move calculations of possible variations. The amount of calculation that's necessary varies according to the character of the position.

In the following chapters, we divide chess strategy into understandable lessons.

"All men can see these
tactics whereby I conquer,
but what none can see is
the strategy out of which
victory is evolved."

—Sun Tzu

—Level II—

Lesson Eight

Strategy– Minor Pieces

In this lesson, you'll learn about the strategic considerations of "good" and "bad" bishops, bishops of opposite color, bishop versus knight, and cutting off pieces from the game.

In this chapter, we'll focus on the strategic elements related to the minor pieces—the bishops and knights.

Good and bad bishops

At the start of a game, all the bishops must certainly be valued equally. But as the position changes, the worth of each bishop can change. The *activity* of a bishop greatly depends on the location of the pawns. A bishop that is *not* blocked by its own pawns is called a *good bishop*, while a *bad bishop* is one whose mobility is severely limited by its own pawns (and sometimes the opponent's pawns too). The following principle of interaction between the pawns and the bishop was formulated by third World Champion, and perhaps the greatest player of all time, José Raúl Capablanca:

When your opponent has a bishop, you should place your pawns on the same color squares as the bishop (travels on). However, if you have a bishop yourself, then you should try to keep the pawns on different colored squares than your bishop (travels on), no matter if your opponent has a bishop or not.

Of course, the general correctness of these principles does not mean that we should follow them dogmatically. We will demonstrate later how these principles are malleable, depending on the need of the position.

Precisely defining good and bad bishops is not so easy. But, to paraphrase U.S. Supreme Court Justice Potter Stewart, who was admittedly speaking on quite a different subject—we can't define a bad bishop, but we know one when we see it. Let's look at an example.

Alatortsev—Levenfish
Tbilisi, 1937

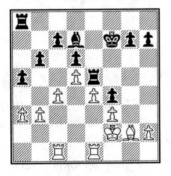

After 25. Kf2

All but one of the black pawns are located on dark squares, while most of the white pawns and the bishops of both sides are located on light squares.

There is a noticeable difference in the activity of the bishops: the black bishop on d7 is definitely a *good bishop*. Its movement is not obstructed by its own pawns and it protects the light squares from enemy invaders. This bishop and its own pawns complement each other in

controlling both light and dark squares. In particular, black controls e5, an important central square that cannot be attacked by a white bishop or pawn.

White's bishop on g2 can be condemned as a *bad bishop* because its movement is greatly restricted by its own pawns. White's position contains weak dark squares because neither his pawns nor his bishop is able to protect them.

Based on these factors, we can conclude that black's position is *strategically better.* Thus black should be able to develop a plan that realizes the advantages inherent in the position.

25. ... Kf6 26. Ke2 Rh5! (The rook finds an even more active position.) **27. Rh1 Ke5!**

Black centralizes his king for the endgame—a useful technique to remember! Black's bishop controls many squares, while white's counterpart is "a tall pawn." Likewise, black's rooks are more active than white's. All these advantages add up to excellent winning chances for black. (He did indeed go on to win the game.)

**Botvinnik—Kan
Leningrad, 1939**

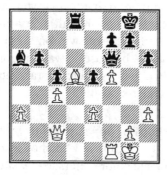

After 25. ... axb6

Some positions with bishops that would ordinarily be considered *good* or *bad* by the usual criteria require a more subtle evaluation. It is not always quite as simple as placing your pawns on the opposite color of your bishop.

26. e4

This turns out to be the best move on the board, anchoring white's attacking pawn on f5 and freeing up white's rook from defensive duties, while giving extra protection to white's bishop.

But white puts another pawn on a white square, cutting off his bishop from his side of the board—does that make it a bad bishop?

No! From its protected position on d5, the bishop exerts power from the center toward both enemy flanks. So it cannot be considered bad. It can't protect its king, but here such defense isn't a very important consideration. The range and impact of the bishop's activity from d5 is greater than it would be from any other square—for example, it would be more restricted and less effective on d3. Black's bishop, facing impenetrable barriers on all sides, is much more restricted than white's. The position must be evaluated as better for white.

Let's briefly look at how white capitalized on his advantage.

26. ... Bc8

26 .... b5 leads to the loss of

It is not always quite as simple as placing your pawns on the opposite color of your bishop.

the c5-pawn after 27. cxb5 Bxb5 28. Rb1.

27. Qa4 Bd7 28. Qa7 Be8

Black must protect his pawn on f7, which is attacked by white's queen and bishop. (It should be clear by now that white's bishop, although blocked by his pawns on c4 and e4, is not at all "bad"!) Furthermore, white's queen on a7 and the half open b-file point to another weakness in black's position—his b6-pawn.

29. Rb1 Rd6 30. a4

The objective here is to weaken the two-pawn chain at its base (an important strategic technique), making the black pawn on c5 vulnerable. This maneuver will soon win a pawn.

30. ... Kh7 31. a5 bxa5 32. Qxa5

Now nothing can protect the c5-pawn. White went on to win it and the game:

32. ... Ra6 33. Qxc5 Ra2 34. Qe3 Qa6 35. Rb8 Qa4 36. Kh2 Ra3 37. Qc5 Ra2 38. Ra8 Qxa8 39. Bxa8 Rxa8 40. Qxe5 Bc6 41. Qc7 1–0

The main point to remember from this game is that the white bishop remained a tower of strength, even though every one of white's pawns was on a light-square—because it was in front of the pawns, able to rake the defender's position.

Bishops of opposite color

The phrase "bishops of opposite color" refers to any situation in which each side has only one bishop, and these two bishops move on different color squares. Later, we'll see that, in the endgame, this condition tends to result in a significantly larger percentage of draws—even when one side is ahead a pawn or even two. But in the middlegame, bishops of opposite color can result in a player being weak on the color squares not covered by his bishop, or especially strong on the squares his bishop does cover.

Bishops of opposite color can be drawish in the endgame.

In such positions, when one side's bishop can coordinate with other friendly pieces to initiate an attack, the defense can be very difficult, because the defender is, in effect, a piece down on one color complex of squares—either dark or light. The bishop of the defending side cannot participate fully in the fight.

Matulovich—Botvinnik
Belgrade, 1970

Black to move

In the diagram above, black is a pawn down, but he is on move, his king is safe, and his dark-squared bishop glares menacingly at the b2-square near the white king. The presence of opposite-color bishops offers him a successful attack on the dark squares. On the other hand,

white's bishop bites on the granite of the black king's pawn shelter. Thus, black is clearly better. In fact, he has several moves that would win: 1. ... Qb6 (actually played), 1. ... Rc8, and 1. ... c3. The most direct win would have been to attack a1 with the queen.

1. ... Qa7! 2. Re2

If 2. Kb1, then 2. ... c3! 3. bxc3 Ra8 4. Kc1 Qa1+ 5 Kd2 Rd8+ 6 Ke2 Re8+ and white loses major material.

2. ... Qa1+!

2. ... Ra8 also works.

3. Bb1 c3!

4. bxc3 Qa3+ 5. Kc2 Qa4+ 6. Kb2 Qxb4+

But for the attacker, owning an opposite-color bishop can be like having an extra piece!

7. Kc2 Qa4+ 8. Kb2 Rb8+
9. Kc1 Qa3+ 10. Kc2 Qb2+

that the bishop and knight excel in different kinds of positions. This makes perfect sense because the bishop and knight have very different capabilities. Let's briefly contrast them:

Bishop	Knight
Long range	Short range
Moves along diagonals	Jumps in L-shape
Stays on only one color	Alternates color with each move

11. Kd3 Qxc3+ 12. Ke4 Qd4#

In this example, white was helpless on the black squares in front of his king because of the effect of the bishops of opposite color.

Bishop versus knight

Because minor pieces—the bishops and knights—are considered of approximately equal value at the start of a game, they're frequently exchanged for each other in the middlegame. But it's important to understand

It's true that, knowing nothing else about a specific position, almost all masters would choose to have a bishop against a knight. But the devil is always in details. Let's take a look at some examples that show the contrasting capabilities of the two pieces.

A. Zaitsev—Spassky
1960

White to move

1. h5!

White, a pawn down but with open files for his rooks and control of the long dark diagonal, must attack while black's pieces are disorganized and his knight out of play.

1. ... b4

With this move, black tries, but fails, to remove the bishop from the all-important diagonal. Better defense is offered by 1. ... Rd7 or 1. ... c4.

2. hxg6 hxg6

2. ... bxc3 3. gxf7++, with mate in two.

3. Rd6 Kh7

Defending against the capture on g6.

4. Qc4, black resigns

Black's short-range knight never had a chance to get into the game. Now if 4. ... Qxc4?, the black queen would be *deflected* from the defense of h1, permitting 5. Rh1+ Kg8 6. Rh8#. All

other tries fail as well—for example: 4. ... f5 5. Qxe4 (5. Qf1 also wins) 5. ... fxe4 6. Rh1+ Kg8 7. Rh8+ Kf7 8. Rf6+.

Karpov—Taimanov
1983

After 35. ... R8c7

This position, on the other hand, highlights a superior knight. White occupies the important central squares d4 and e5. The black bishop on b7 is limited in mobility by his own pawns. Even though black has taken control of the c-file, gained entrance to white's second rank, and, importantly, is up a pawn—white's position is still better!

Karpov decides to exchange dark-squared bishops (leaving him with a superior knight against an inferior bishop) and transfer his knight to d4, pressuring the e6-pawn. In this case, even the exchange of queens will not ease black's defense.

36. Nf3 Kh8 37. Bxg7+ Qxg7

**38. Nd4! Qxg3 39. hxg3 R2c3
40. Nxe6 Rc8 41. Kh2**

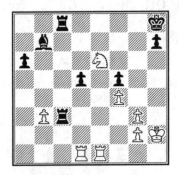

41. ... Rxb3

Black could try 41. ... d4, seizing the opportunity to activate his bishop.

42. Nd4

The bishop, with only two available moves, can't protect the f-pawn.

**42. ... Rb6 43. Nxf5 Rf8
44. Nd4 Rg8**

The perfect knight fully dominates the bishop.

**45. Re7 Rg7 46. Rde1 Rh6+
47. Kg1 Rhg6**

48. f5 Rb6

If 48. ... Rxg3, then 49. f6! Rxg2+ 50. Kh1. And if 48. ... Rf6, then white will continue with 49. g4!.

49. R7e6

The rest is easy.

49. ... Rxe6

On 49. ... Rb2, 50. Re8+ Rg8 51. f6 ends it.

**50. fxe6 Rg8 51. e7 Re8 52. Nf5
Bc6 53. Nd6 Rg8 54. e8Q Bxe8
55. Nxe8 Rxg3 56. Nf6, black
resigns.**

If 56. ... d4 or 56. ... Rg5, then 57. Re7—threatening the Arabian mate!

An amazing cavalry raid—of the last 20 moves, the white knight made 10 of them, conducting half of the game by itself! In contrast, the poor black bishop never found a way to get into the game, ultimately sacrificing itself for the promoted white f-pawn.

Cutting off a piece from the main action

The final strategic consideration regarding minor pieces we'll look at in this chapter is cutting off a knight or bishop from the fray. (Occasionally such a disaster may entrap a rook or even a queen.) Obviously, that can leave one player effectively up a piece. Take a look at this example.

White to move

1. e5!

White cuts off black's bishop, giving himself an easy win. The following play shows him soon playing on the queenside a pawn up:

1. ... Bh6 2. Nd4 Kf7 3. Nc6 a6

4. a4 Ke8 5. a5 Kd7 6. Nb8+ Kc7 7. Nxa6+

White has an easy win. His opponent's bishop is "thinking" strictly "inside the box"!

Here's another example:

White or black to move

The situation is even worse for black and it makes no difference who is to move. His bishop has no safe move at all, and his king can't get out of its prison without sacrificing his bishop. White wins by simply marching his king up the board to c6 and moving his bishop to f4 (or b4) to double attack the black pawn on d6, winning it—allowing him to queen his own d-pawn.

The two extreme examples above show a bishop being shut out of the main action of a game. But it can happen to a knight as well.

White or black to move

In the diagram above, the bishop has the enemy knight corralled on the edge of the board, where the knight is traditionally weakest. The "X's" mark the potential moves for the knight, and we can see that they are all covered by the bishop.

If the knight could safely hop into the game, white could draw without problems. But with the knight out of play, black wins easily by simply advancing his pawn: 1. Ke2 g5! 2. Kd2 g4!, preventing 3. Nc3, because after 3. ... Bxc3+ 4. Kxc3 g3, the pawn queens.

Let's look at a more complicated position, from a game between two amateurs competing in a tournament.

Official USCF Ratings
Master = 2200 and up
Expert = 2000-2199
Class A = 1800-1999
Class B = 1600-1799
Class C = 1400-1599
Class D = 1200-1399
—and so on—

**Cobb (USCF rating 1293)—
Moore (USCF rating 1692)
2010**

After 10. a3

By move 10, Matt Cobb, as white, playing against a much higher-rated competitor, had already achieved a somewhat better game. At that point, black played a terrible move.

10. ... Ba6?

The idea of exchanging the passive c8-bishop for white's good one is correct, but not its implementation.

Cobb wrote: "I will lock up the black queen's rook, knight, and bishop, hold e5, and move my pieces kingside for the attack."

11. b5 Bc8

Here was the last moment black could (and should) get two pawns for a piece: 11. ... bxc5! 12. bxa6 c4—but even here white is winning!

12. c6 Nb8

Now 13. Ne5, followed by the attack with g2-g4-g5, wins quickly and easily. Cobb instead played 13. Be5—also leaving him with an easy win—and he indeed won without facing any serious problems.

We've looked at some of the most important strategies involving the minor pieces. In the next chapter, we'll examine strategic considerations concerning the major pieces.

Steinitz's Four Rules

1. The right to attack belongs to the side that has a positional advantage, and that side not only has the right to attack but also the obligation to do so, or else his advantage could evaporate. The attack should be concentrated on the weakest square in the opponent's position.

2. If in an inferior position, the defender should be ready to defend and make compromises, or take other measures, such as a desperate counterattack.

3. In an equal position, the opponents should maneuver, trying to achieve a position in which they have an advantage. If both sides play correctly, an equal position will remain equal.

4. The advantage may be a big, indivisible one (for example, a rook on the seventh rank), or it may be a whole series of small advantages. The goal of the stronger side is to store up the advantages, and to convert temporary advantages into permanent ones.

Level I, Lesson Two
Memory Markers!

White to move

Black to move

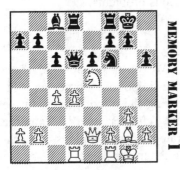

After 1. ... Bh3

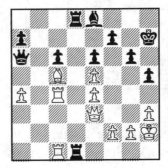

Black to move

White to move

White to move

Solutions:

MM1: 1. c5!. Although this move relinquishes white's control over the d5 square, it is clearly best, since it is a life sentence for the prisoner on c8. Besides, the d6-square is more important for white than the d5-square is for black. (Palatnik—Dandridge, 1996)

MM2: Evaluate the position. Black is lost. The game Rubinstein—Spielmann, 1926, ended after 1. ... Rxc1 2. Bf8, but even the stronger 1. ... Kg7 does not save black—for example, 2. Rxd1 Rxd1 3. Rd4 Qf1 4. Rxd1 Qxd1 5. Qg5 Qd7 6. Qf6+ Kg8 7. Be3 Kh7 8. h4, with the threat of Bh6.

MM3: 2. e4!. Facing the prospect of an exchange of bishops, white changes the pawn structure, closing the diagonal for the g2-bishop and preparing for a pawn assault with f2-f4. This negates the value of its exchange. Now if black reconsiders trading and retreats his bishop to e6 or d7, losing two tempos, then f2-f4 will follow, with better play for white. White stands better. (Petrosian—Gheorghiu, 1967)

MM4: 1. ... e4!. After 2. Bxf6 Qxf6 3. fxe4, black plays 3. ... f4!, with 4. ... Ne5 to follow. Black then has a powerful knight against a bad bishop, and good chances for a pawn storm on the kingside. (Pilnik—Geller, 1955)

MM5: 1. Rxg7+!. After **1. ... Kxg7 2. Rg1+ Kh8** (2. ... Kf6 3. Qh4+ Kf5 4. Rg5+ Kf6 5. Rxe5+ Kg6 6. Rg5 mate; 2. ... Kh6 3. Qh4 mate) **3. Qxe5+** (the diagonal is wide open!) **3. ... dxe5 4. Bxe5+ f6** (the last interference) **5. Bxf6+!**, and mate next move. (Hartford—Aficio, 1887)

MM6: 1. Rxh4 Qxh4 (if 1. ... Nxh4 2. Bg5, with a promising attack) **2. Qxh4 Nxh4 3. Nb6 Rb8** (the rook would stand even worse on a7) **4. Bf4 Nf5** (if 4. ... Rd8, 5. c5) **5. d5**, the point of the combination. Black's queenside is semi-paralyzed. White stands better. (Anand—Ivanchuk, 1996)

**"However beautiful
the strategy, you should
occasionally look at
the results."**

—Winston Churchill

—Level II—

Lesson Nine

Strategy– Major Pieces

*In this lesson, you'll learn to create and exploit
open and semi-open files, and
to use outposts on such files.*

The major or "heavy" pieces, queens and rooks, can effectively show their strength on both open and semi-open files. An *open file* is one which is entirely free of pawns. A *half-open* or *semi-open* file is one free of your own pawns, but which still contains one or more of the opponent's pawns. For example, after 1. e4 c5 2. Nf3 d6 3. d4 cxd4 4. Nxd4:

Black has the semi-open c-file.
White has the semi-open d-file.

Each side has a semi-open file and is already thinking of ways to put a rook on these files. For rooks are like naval destroyers in dry dock unless they are placed on a semi-open or open file.

The main objective of any operation on an open file is the eventual occupation of the 7th or 8th rank.
—Aaron Nimzovich

Exploiting control of an open file

Your rooks in particular have one ultimate goal—to get to the enemy's first or second rank (what the old masters called the "seventh" or "eighth" ranks). Open files represent the main road to this goal.

Meduna—Palatnik
Frunze, 1979

Black to move

Black's control over the open b-file serves as his gateway to the enemy camp.

1. ... Rb8! 2. Bd1 Bxd1

The exchange of the light-squared bishops does not ease the pressure on the b-file.

3. Rxd1 Qb3 4. Ra1 Qb2 5. Ra2 Qxd2 6. Rxd2

Black's only remaining heavy piece is enough to control the b-file.

6. ... Rb3 7. Ra2

The black rook attacks; the white rook only defends.

7. ... Nd7

Black's knight heads for the queenside to get into the fray.

8. Kf3 (White will use his king to try to cover up his weaknesses.**)**
8. ... Nb6 9. Ke2 (If instead 9. a4, black would play 9. ... a5 and 10. ... Rb4, winning the a-pawn.**)**
9. ... Na4 10. Kd2 Rb1!

Despite the reduced material, white remains cramped. His pieces are passive and unable to create any threats. Additionally, the white king unexpectedly turns out to be unsafe. For example, if 11. f4?, then 11. ... Nc3 12. Rc2 Rd1 mate.

Analysis after 12. ... Rd1#.
The Hook Mate pattern in practice!

11. Nc2 Rf1! (winning a pawn) **12. Ke2 Rh1 13. Ra1**

White doesn't have time for 13. h4, saving the pawn, because a bigger threat, 13. ... Nc3+, must be defused.

We've already shown the power of exploiting the open file and could stop here. But let's continue until the end—it's a beautifully played, instructive, and very practical endgame.

13. ... Rxh2 14. Kf3 g5 15. Nb4 (white's move is as good as anything he has). **15. ... g4+!**

Very practical! Black plays a deflecting sacrifice in order to take the knight in comfort. It's trickier to take the knight right away: 15. ... cxb4 16. axb4 Nb2? (16. ... Nc3 is better) 17. Ke2, and black has lost much of his advantage.

16. Kxg4 cxb4 17. axb4 Nb2 18. Ra3 Rxf2 19. b5 axb5 20. cxb5 Nd1

Finally, black is able to use his extra knight to weave a mating net.

21. Rb3 Ne3+ 22. Kh3 f5!

White resigns because of the threat of 23. ... Ng4 and 24. ... Rh2#. If 23. g4 fxg4+ 24. Kh4 Rf3 25. Kh5 Kg7, and then 26. ... Rh3 mate.

**Steiner—Botvinnik
Groningen, 1946**

After 24. Qxf4

We've already seen examples of the use of the semi-open file to attack the king—for example, Spassky—Evans, Varna, 1962 (in the lesson "Attack and Defense"). Botvinnik's opponent Herman Steiner was well known in the 1940s and 1950s as the leader of the Hollywood Chess Group, headquartered in a clubhouse next to the Steiner residence, attracting major movie stars like Humphrey Bogart and Lauren Bacall.

24. ... Rg4 25. Qd2 Nh4

Black ignores the pawn, exploiting the de facto semi-open h-file—his heavy pieces are in front of the h-pawn.

26. Ne3 (if 26. Nxh4, then 26. ... Rxh4 is lethal—for example, 27.h3 Rxh3+ 28.Bxh3 Qxh3#) **26. ... Nxf3 27. exf3** (27. Bxf3 Qxh2+ 28. Kxh2 Rh4#) **27. ... Rh4 28. Nf1**

28. ... Bg5 0–1

Black intends to follow up with ... Bf4 and checkmate on h2.

Fighting for control of the open file

In the diagram below, the b-file is again open, but not under control as yet by either player. The player who gains control of it will have an advantage.

**Bronstein—Boleslavsky
Candidates Playoff, 1950**

After 21. ... Rxa6

Many masters would simply play 22. Rfb1! here and would indeed claim an advantage. If that was your reaction as well, you found a master-level move. But David Bronstein was a highly unorthodox and original thinker and player. Here he found:

22. Qc5!

White doesn't mind if his pawns become disconnected and doubled, since the prize is full control of the only open file.

22. ... Rb8 23. Rfb1

23. ... Qxc5

If 23. ... Rab6, 24. Rxb6 Rxb6 25. c4

Analysis: Position after 25. c4

At the right moment, white breaks down the stone wall facing his bishop.

24. dxc5 Kf8

25. Rb5 (the b5-outpost secures white's dominance on the b-file; more on outposts later in this section.) **25. ... Raa8 26. Kf2**

Capturing on b5 isn't a good option for black. So white has all the time he needs to improve the position of his king, and then open a second front on the kingside. Opening a second front is a technique often required to press an advantage in a position like this—with a clear advantage on one side of the board, but no means to translate it into something meaningful, like a material

superiority. White won this ending after a grueling 41 more
moves!

Taking the square on your
opponent's back rank under control is often enough to grab the
open file.

White to move

How should white play here?
Of course, 1. Ba6!, and the c-file
is his! But if instead it's black to
move, and if he plays 1. ... Bb7,
we're following a grandmaster
game:

Geller—Simagin
Moscow, 1951

After 15. ... Rc8

16. Ba6 (anyway!) **16. ... Bxa6**

17. Qxa6 Rxc1 18. Rxc1 Qa8

So white controls the key
square at the base of the file.
What next?

19. Bd6 Rd8 20. e5

White plays this move only
now, with his bishop already on
d6! (Recall our discussions of
good bishop versus bad bishop.)

20. ... Bg7 21. Rc7

With simple, easy-to-find
moves, white has achieved an
overwhelming position. Black's
only chance is a counterattack,

but with minimal accuracy on white's part, this counterattack should fail.

21. ... Qe4 (black's best practical chance) **22. Nd2 Qe1+** (22. ... Qxd4 23.Rxd7) **23. Nf1 Nf8 24. Qxa7 Bh6**

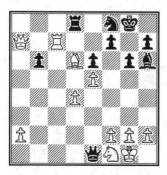

25. Rxf7 and in a few more moves, black resigned.

Exploiting a semi-open file

Operating on a semi-open file, you should consider:

a. Opening it at the right moment;

b. Creating an enemy backward pawn on the file and then attacking it.

Let's look at how the great Cuban champion José Raúl Capablanca brilliantly exploits the potential of the half-open file and adjoining ranks in a classic encounter.

**Nimzovich—Capablanca
New York, 1927**

26. ... Ne7

Avoiding the premature exchange of knights and transferring his own knight to the kingside. The big question here is whether or not, or rather, how much, black can profit from ownership of the semi-open file.

27. Red2 Rc4 28. Qh3

The queen has little to do on h3. The best place for her majesty is f2.

28. ... Kg7 29. Rf2 a5 (expanding on the queenside) **30. Re2 Nf5 31. Nxf5+.**

Taking the square on your opponent's back rank under control is often enough to grab the open file.

31. ... gxf5

Black's control of the half-open c-file and of the fourth rank gives him good winning chances.

32. Qf3 (if 32. Qxh5 Rh8 33. Qf3 Rh4) **32. ... Kg6 33. Red2 Re4!**

34. Rd4 Rc4

Black sneaks another rook into white's camp through the fourth rank.

35. Qf2 Qb5 36. Kg3 (36. Rxc4 offers stiffer defense, but black would remain with an advantage.)

36. ... Rcxd4 37. cxd4 Qc4 38. Kg2

Through his purposeful play, black has taken control of the c-file, now completely open, while placing his rook within the enemy camp.

38. ... b5

Improving his position without allowing any counterplay.

39. Kg1 b4 40. axb4 axb4 41. Kg2 Qc1 42. Kg3 Qh1

White is in *Zugzwang*.

43. Rd3 Re1 (a decisive infiltration) **44. Rf3 Rd1 45. b3 Rc1**

46. Re3 (46. Kh3 Rc2) **46. ... Rf1 47. Qe2 Qg1+ 48. Kh3 Rf2 0–1**

A masterpiece, and an exemplary demonstration of how to use open and semi-open files and ranks.

Creating a semi-open file

In the example below, neither player has a semi-open file, so black creates one!

**Matisons—Nimzovich
Carlsbad, 1929**

18. ... a6! 19. bxa6 Rxa6

Black has pried open the a-file, pressuring white's isolated a-pawn, while his knight occupies an outpost on c4 that guards his own backward pawn along the b-file.

Now both black's rook pair and his knight pair are ready to harass—and soon start winning—weak white pawns (on a2 and c3), while white has no way to effectively use the semi-open b-file, nor the semi-open d-file he creates after 20. dxc5 bxc5.

**20. dxc5 bxc5 21. Ng2 Nd5
22. Rd3 Rfa8**

23. e4 Ne5 0–1

The black knights trample white's position.

Exploiting an outpost on an open file

When struggling for control of the open file, an outpost (a square protected by your pawn which can't be attacked by your opponent's pawns or minor pieces), can be a great asset. We're going to take a look at a masterful illustration of this done on a very high level of competition by Reuben Fine.

Reuben Fine, one of the two strongest American players in the 1930s, turned down an invitation to the world championship tournament in 1948, at least in part because he feared that Soviet players would throw games to each other. Ironically, in this next

example, he defeats the Russian who would go on to win that tournament and the throne.

**Fine—Botvinnik
Amsterdam, 1938**

White to move

Here the white rook on d6 occupies an important outpost, located on the open file. Behind this outpost, white regroups his forces, first winning the isolated a-pawn.

**22. Qe3 Ra7 23. Nd2 a3 24. c4
Ba4 25. exf6 Qxf6 26. Rxa3 Re8
27. h3**

White's last move underlines

his decisive advantage. Black has no counterplay. Besides, white's knight is stronger than black's restricted bishop. (Recall Lesson 8.) The knight will soon move into the center of the board, where it radiates power.

27. ... Raa8 28. Nf3 Qb2 29. Ne5 Qb1+ 30. Kh2 Qf5 31. Qg3, black resigns.

White threatens a crushing 32. Rd7. If 31. ... Ra7, 32. Nxc6 (pin!); if 31. ... Rf8, 32. Nd7 and then Nb6 (fork!); and if 31. ... Re7, 32. Rxa4 (deflection!). A strategic masterpiece!

Creating an outpost on a semi-open file

This next example shows a win by perhaps the strongest player of the late 19th century. Siegbert Tarrasch was by profession a doctor. His prescription here is to create an outpost on the semi-open d-file.

Tarrasch — Blackburne
Manchester, 1890

After 9. ... Ne8

White, with more space (e4 vs. d6) and harmoniously placed pieces, clearly stands better.

10. Nd5 Nxd4 11. Bxd7 Qxd7 (Not 11. ... Nxc2 12. Bxe8 Nxa1 13. Bb5) **12. Qxd4 Bd8 13. Rad1 Qe6 14. Qd3**

14. ... c6

Black's patience has come to an end, and he decides to push the white knight away from the outpost on d5. But this weakens the d6-pawn, which becomes backward.

15. Ne3 f6 (On 15. ... Bf6, 16. Ba3 puts more pressure on d6.) **16. Nf5 Bc7 17. Rfe1 Rd8 18. c4**

Fixing the weakness on d6. It is now hard to imagine that the backward d-pawn will ever advance. White's position is much better.

18. ... Rf7 19. Qh3 Kh8?

White's threat was 20. Nh6+. Black needed to move his queen to c8 or d7 to save her and to avoid the following combination that wins the Exchange.

20. Nh6! Qxh3 (Or 20. ... Re7 21. Qxe6 Rxe6 22. Nf7+) **21. Nxf7+ Kg8 22. gxh3 Kxf7 23. f4** And white went on to win. Strictly speaking, both d5 and f5 were not outposts because the white knight could be driven away from them by enemy pawns—but only at a high cost!

Level II, Lesson Nine
Memory Markers!

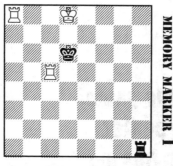

White to move

White to move

White to move

Black to move

Solutions:

MM1: **1. Rh5!**, winning. If 1. ... Rxh5, 2. Ra6+ and 3. Ra5+.

MM2: White is much better; for instance, he can snatch the b-pawn. But **1. c5** is even stronger. After **1. ... Rfe8 2. Rfd1**, determined to control the d-file, white got a decisive edge. (Botvinnik—Szabo, 1956)

MM3: Hint: Open the files! **1. Bxg6!** 1:0. If 1. ... Rb6, 2. Bxh7+ and 3. Qxb6. (Pillsbury—Wolf, 1903)

MM4: **1. ... a5! 2. a3 Ra6!!**. Black prepares to double or even triple on the a-file, threatening to open it at the right moment. (Vasiliev—Zilberstein, 1993)

"Chess is a terrible game.
If you have no center,
your opponent has a
freer position.
If you do have a center,
then you really have
something to worry about!"

—Siegbert Tarrasch

—Level II—

Lesson Ten

Strategy— Significance of the Center

In this lesson, you'll learn the advantages of a strong pawn center, and how to undermine, both with pawns and pieces, a shaky pawn center.

Control of the center is the most important element in chess strategy. The center of the chess board is formed by the squares e4, e5, d4, d5. The so-called *expanded center* also includes the squares within the rectangle enclosing c3, c6, f3 and f6.

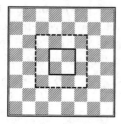

The center and expanded center

From the very first moves, the chess struggle revolves around the center. Pawns and pieces are more active and have greater potential in the center. From their central positions, they may have a great influence on the opponent's position and limit his choices.

White is usually on the offensive in the struggle for the center—he can be first to advance a center pawn. Black's strategy early in the game often amounts simply to neutralizing white's first-move advantage by claiming his own share of the center.

The strong pawn center

The "classic" pawn formation in the center is the duo d4 + e4 (for black, it's d5 + e5). If the central pawns are strong and well protected, then the pawn center is a positional advantage. But if the pawns are weak and can be objects of attack, then this kind of center can be a serious liability.

In many modern openings, black simply allows white to create a strong pawn center, and in return gets the chance to undermine it. In such cases, the power of the center often depends on its ability to advance, as in the following example.

Polugaevsky—Tal
Moscow, 1969

After 7. bxc3

7. ... cxd4 (Black is cramped, so he wants to exchange a pair of bishops and quickly castle into safety.) **8. cxd4 Bb4+ 9. Bd2**

9. ... Bxd2+

After 9. ... Qa5 10. Rb1 Bxd2+ 11. Qxd2 Qxd2+ 12. Kxd2

White is better. Here, as in most other endgames in an early phase (with many pieces still on the board), the center pawns trump the pawns on the flank. Also note how well-placed the white king will be on e3, practically in the center but still very safe. By the way, black's 12th move will be ... Ke7, to keep his

If the central pawns are strong and well protected, then the pawn center is a positional advantage.

king in the center for the ending, rather than ... 0–0?, which would be more suitable if queens were still on the board.

10. Qxd2 0–0 11. Bc4 Nc6 12. 0–0 b6

13. Rad1

With this move, white indicates his decision to play along the central e- and d-files and the kingside, rather than in the center and queenside (in that case, his a-rook would go to c1).

13. ... Bb7 14. Rfe1 Na5 15. Bd3 Rc8

In this position (often played in those days), Polugaevsky unleashed a surprise, transforming his classic center into a classic attack.

16. d5 exd5 17. e5 Nc4 18. Qf4

Black is up a pawn, but his position is difficult, as all white pieces are aimed at his king. (And note how truly bad black's bishop on b7 is.)

But if the center pawns are weak and can be attacked, then they can be a serious liability

18. ... Nb2 19. Bxh7+ (A familiar combination!) **19. ... Kxh7 20. Ng5+ Kg6** (20. ... Kg8 21. Qh4) **21. h4 Rc4**

22. h5+ Kh6

22. ... Kxh5 23. g4+ would result in various checkmates—find them!

23. Nxf7++ Kh7 (23. ... Kxh5 24. Qf5+) **24. Qf5+ Kg8 25. e6 Qf6** (25. ... Nxd1 loses to both 26. e7 and 26. h6) **26. Qxf6 gxf6**

White is much better. His e6-pawn is worth more than black's bishop. White won after:

27. Rd2! Rc6 (27. ... Na4 28. Nd6 Bc6 29. e7 Re8 30. Nxe8 Bxe8 31. Rxd5) **28. Rxb2**

28. ... Re8

Black could offer a stiffer defense with 28. ... Bc8, but it still loses.

29. Nh6+ Kh7 30. Nf5 Rexe6 31. Rxe6 Rxe6 32. Rc2

White gains "his" open file, plus a clear-cut case of good knight versus bad bishop!

32. ... Rc6 33. Re2 Bc8 34. Re7+ Kh8 35. Nh4 f5

Defending against 36. Ng6+ and 37. h6.

36. Ng6+ Kg8 37. Rxa7 1–0

It's hopeless for black. He will be forced to give up more material in order to avoid the knight, rook and pawn mates.

White threatens two checkmates.

Undermining your opponent's center

White's perfect center is composed of pawns on e4 and d4. To undermine even this ideal center, however, often all black needs to do is to force one of these pawns to move. The following game shows black using the "hypermodern" strategic technique of ceding a large center to white, and then battling to undermine it.

Gligoric—Smyslov
Kiev, 1959

**1. d4 Nf6 2. c4 g6 3. Nc3 d5
4. cxd5 Nxd5 5. e4 Nxc3 6. bxc3**

In this main line of the Gruenfeld Defense, white gets a strong center. In exchange, black gets a quick, harmonious development and opportunities to pressure the center.

**6. ... Bg7 7. Bc4 c5 8. Ne2 0–0
9. 0–0 Nc6 10. Be3 Qc7 11. Rc1
Rd8**

12. h3 (to be able to play f2-f4 without allowing ... Bg4) **12. ...
b6 13. f4 e6 14. Qe1 Bb7**

15. Qf2 (ready to play 16. f5, but
…) **15. … Na5 16. Bd3**

16. … f5!

Attacking—and trying to fix,
that is, to immobilize—white's
extended center.

17. e5 c4 18. Bc2 Nc6

Now black is dominant
everywhere: in the center (his
control of d5 is important and
offers a perfect outpost for the
knight), on the kingside (black's
king is much safer than white's),
and especially on the queenside
(where he's a pawn up).

19. g4 (this attack does white

more harm than good) **19. …
Ne7 20. Kh2 Qc6 21. Ng3 b5
22. a4 a6 23. Rb1 Rab8 24. Bd2**

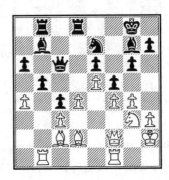

**24. … bxa4 25. Ra1 Ba8
26. Bxa4 Qc7 27. Ra2 Rb6
28. gxf5**

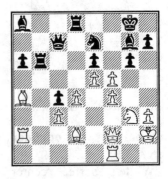

29. … exf5!!

White's two connected, protected passed pawns on d4 and e5
are of little value, while the
opening of the g-file (with 29. …
gxf5) would give white some
counter-play.

**29. Bc1 Nd5 30. Ne2 a5 31. Bc2
Rb3!**

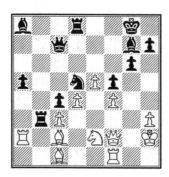

Black finds a helpful tactic.

32. Bxb3 cxb3 33. Ra4 Bf8 (activating the dark-square bishop) **34. Bb2 Ne3**

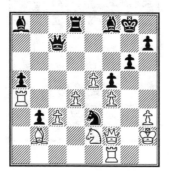

More tactics—which often flow from a superior position!

35. Rfa1

If 35. Qxe3?, black plays 35. ... Qc6, double-attacking the rook on a4 and the checkmating square on g2.

35. ... Nc4 36. Ng3 Be7 37. Nf1 Qc6 38. Rxc4

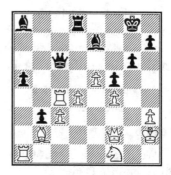

Often beautiful lines "stay in the notes": If instead 38. Ng3, black could play 38. ... Nxb2 39. Qxb2 Bh4 40. Nh1 Be1!—a wonderful deflection sacrifice. White must capture the bishop to prevent mate on h1, and black will snare the rook on a4.

38. ... Qh1+ 39. Kg3 h5 0–1

It's mate in two.

A marvelous performance by former world champion Vasily Smyslov. But note that the technique he uses of encouraging white to build a big center requires a deep strategic understanding. A less experienced player could be quickly over-

The technique of encouraging white to build a big center requires a deep strategic understanding.

whelmed by such a big center. Nevertheless, the center-challenging techniques used above are very practical and instructive.

Let's look at the beginning of another grandmaster game that shows the center-undermining techniques in a different opening.

Ivanovic—Gurevich
Lucerne, 1989

1. e4 d6 2. d4 Nf6

We'll learn later that this is called the Pirc Defense.

3. Nc3 g6 4. f4 Bg7 5. e5

8. dxc5 Qa5! 9. Be2 Bxc3+ 10. bxc3 Qxc3+ 11. Bd2 Qxc5 12. dxe7

12. … Re8!

With a better game for black, who went on to win.

Pieces versus the pawn center

A proud center can some-

5. … Nfd7! (preparing to undermine white's center) **6. Nf3 c5!** (undermining begins!) **7. exd6 0–0!**

A proud center can sometimes be attacked by pieces alone.

times be attacked by pieces alone. In the game below, we can see how future world champion Mikhail Tal, as black, resists weakening his "perfect" center by moving either his d5 or e5 pawn. But his opponent skillfully applies pressure with pieces to both the center pawns and to black's king position, with devastating effect.

Nezmetdinov—Tal
Moscow, 1957

After 19. ... fxe5

Black has a central pawn duo, but white will show how shaky it is!

20. Bb5! Bb7

Or 20. ... d4 21. Bc4+ Kh8 22. Qe4, with Rf7 to follow (if 22. ... dxc3, then 23. Qxc6!).

21. Qg3 Rd7 22. Rf2!

22. ... Re8 (22. ... d4? 23. Bc4+ Kh8 24. Rdf1) **23. h3 Ba8 24. Ba4 Bb7 25. Kh1 Ba8 26. Rf5**

26. ... e4

A time-trouble mistake that makes white's task easier. But also bad is 26. ... d4 27. Bb3+ Kh8 28. Rdf1. And after 26. ... g6, white has 27. Rdf1 Rdd8 28. Rf6 Rc8 29. Qf3, with a winning position.

27. Qxc7 Rxc7 28. Rfxd5

Now white's decisive advantage has materialized.

28. ... e3 29. Rd7 e2

This looks dangerous, but ...

30. Bb3+ Re6 31. Bxe6+ Kf8 32. Bxg7+, black resigns

Black gives up just one move before checkmate: 32. ... Ke8 33. Bf7#.

Although in this chapter we ended with examples showing you techniques that successfully overcame a pawn center, don't make the mistake of thinking that every center can be turned into a liability. Often "the center holds"! And, as in Polugaevsky—Tal, sometimes it expands to serve as a springboard for an effective attack.

As you learn more and more about chess, you'll develop a good sense of when a center is solid and when it is shaky. And even when you're up against a solid center, be ready to fight against it before it's used to overwhelm your position!

Level II, Lesson Ten
Memory Markers!

Black to move

Black to move

Black to move

Black to move

Solutions:

MM1: **1. ... d5**. Otherwise, white dominates in the center and is clearly better.

MM2: **1. ... d5**, with a good game. A white attack is unlikely to succeed; if so, his rook is, at least temporarily, misplaced. (Brown—Keres, 1975)

MM3: **1. ... c5! 2. d5 Ne5**. Black is better; so much better that white's best here is to sac a pawn: 3. Nc4 Nxc4 4. bxc4 Bg6 (or 4. ... Nc8) 5. e5!, with reasonable drawing chances. After 3. Rf1? Bg6 4. Ke1 Nc8!!, black eventually won in Botvinnik—Petrosian, 1963.

MM4: **1. ... d5!=**, preventing white from achieving a perfect (d4-e4 duo) center.

"Holes in your opponent's position must be occupied by pieces, not pawns."

—Siegbert Tarrasch

—Level II—

Lesson Eleven

Strategy— Weak & Strong Squares

In this lesson, you'll learn to recognize and exploit weak and strong squares.

A *weak square* is a square inside your territory—usually the fourth or third rank for white, or the fifth or sixth rank for black—which can be safely occupied by an opponent's piece. Thus, by definition, a weak square in your territory can't be attacked by one of your pawns.

In the following illustration, white's knight occupies black's *weak square* on b6. From white's point of view, b6 is a *strong square*, which he has turned into an outpost, an idea you learned in Lesson Nine, for his knight.

Here b6 is a weak square for black and a strong square for white.

If black has neither a knight nor a dark-square bishop to challenge the intruder, b6 is even "weaker."

However, the usefulness of a

One player's weak square is the other player's strong square.

strong square for white and, alternatively, its negative effect on black's position, depends on other elements of the position as well. The following two diagrams make this point clearly.

White wins easily.

Black wins easily.

To double-check our conclusions, try playing these positions out with a friend.

Weak square complexes

A group of weak like-colored squares is called a *weak square complex*. Such a complex often occurs when a fianchettoed bishop (for example, on black's g7) has been traded—especially for a knight, which leaves his white counterpart on the board, ready to help exploit the weak h6-, g7- and (often) f6-squares. In some cases, such a weakness may prove lethal! We see this situation in the next diagram.

Letelier—Smyslov
Havana, 1967

After 77. Rf1

The light squares around the white king are very weak. Please pay attention to the difference in strength of the bishops: black's bishop on f3 is very powerful, while white's c5-bishop accomplishes little. The weakness in white's position enables black to exploit his advantage with a direct attack on white's king.

77. ... a5!

Freeing the rook from prison on the second rank!

78. bxa5 h2+! (in the actual game, white resigned here) **79. Kxh2 Rb8**

There's no defense against ... Rb8-h8-h1, checkmating.

Strategic use of these ideas

Now that you know what weak squares are, you will try to avoid creating them in your camp, unless in doing so you get something more valuable in return. And besides trying to avoid them, part of strategic play is learning to create and take advantage of such weak squares in your opponent's camp—thus making strong squares for your own army deep in enemy territory and occupying them with your pieces—turning them into effective outposts.

Weak Squares Outside an Army's Camp

We usually apply the term *weak square* to a square within one's home half of the board. But in the diagram below, the squares b4 and d4 are definitely weak for black and strong for white. These squares are crying out to be occupied, at the right moment, by white pieces—either the king or knight.

Pfeiffer—Guimard
Dubrovnic, 1950

After 35. Nxc2
The b4-and d4-squares are future
outposts for white's pieces.

We also hope you carry over your knowledge on the topic of bishop versus knight when you analyze this position. White's knight is definitely superior to black's bishop, hemmed in by his own pawns. Pfeiffer used his strong squares and his superior knight to win this endgame.

A square in front of an opponent's isolated pawn is usually a good one to occupy with one of your pieces.

Level II, Lesson Eleven
Memory Markers!

White to move

Black to move

White to move

After 1. f4

White to move

White to move

MEMORY MARKER 1

MEMORY MARKER 2

MEMORY MARKER 3

MEMORY MARKER 4

MEMORY MARKER 5

MEMORY MARKER 6

Solutions:

MM1: **1. c5!**. A multi-purpose move. The first purpose is to attack with (b3)-b4-b5, and the second one is to transfer the knight to the outpost on d6, black's weak spot and white's stronghold. **1. ... a5** (to stop the advance of the b-pawn; but there is plan "B.") **2. Nb1 Qf8 3. Na3 Bd8 4. Nc4 Bc7 5. Nd6**. White stands much better. If black captures on d6 with a bishop, any pawn recapture is fine. (In the game Botvinnik—Flohr, 1936, white, a few moves later, recaptured with exd6, and won.)

MM2: Black is completely lost. She can try to confuse an opponent with 1. ... g4, but then simple 2. Rdf1 wins quickly and easily. (Ranniku—Grinfeld, 1975)

MM3: **1. h3!**, to stop further weakening of light squares—while the new weakness on g3 is of lesser importance, as black has no knights to exploit it effectively. Instead, after 1. Qf3 h3, white was forced to play 2. g3, as 2. g4 loses to 2. ... Qh4.

MM4: Black's best here is **1. ... exf4!?** **2. Bxf4 Ne5**, and his active pieces fully (or almost fully—he's black, after all) compensate for white's static edge. In Flohr—Suetin, 1950, black played natural 1. ... e4, and after 2. Qd2 Nf6 3. Nc2 Qe8 4. Nb5 Qf7 5. Bd4! Ne8 6. Ne3, white's pieces occupied strong squares—with a clear edge. A protected passer on e4 here proves a weakness!

MM5: **1. Rxa7!** White isn't afraid of ...Bxc5, as this would open the key diagonal for him: **1. ... Bxc5** (what else?) **2. Rxc7 Nxc7 3. dxc5 d4** (the only move, but after 4. Qxd4 Qxd4 5. Bxd4, the endgame is won for white).

MM6: **1. Bxb6 Qxb6 2. Nd5** (this knight is much stronger than the black bishop) **2. ... Qd8 3. f4!** (white can't win a pawn: 3. Nxe7+ Qxe7 4. Qxd6 loses to R[any]d8) **3. ... exf4 4. Qxf4 Qd7 5. Qf5! Rcd8 6. Ra3 Qa7 7. Rc3**. White correctly believes that he can get more than winning a pawn back with 7. Nxe7+. In fact, white is dominant everywhere on the board and has at least two very promising plans—on the queenside or on the kingside. He won with a kingside storm. (Fischer—Balbochan, 1962).

Evaluating Pawns

Pawns should not be evaluated only on the basis of *quantity*—that is, just by counting. The *quality* of pawns is a vital consideration. To help you evaluate pawns, here's a simple two-column chart, with brief definitions, that shows you which pawn characteristics are generally strong and which are weak. Of course, the other factors of a position must be taken into consideration in your evaluations of whether pawns are strong or weak, but this is a good general guide:

Strong

Connected: two or more pawns on adjacent files

Passed: a pawn with no enemy pawns on files adjacent to it

Protected passed pawn: a passed pawn protected by a friendly pawn (very strong, unless effectively blockaded!)

Fewer pawn islands: a pawn island is a group of friendly pawns on adjacent files.

Weak

Doubled or tripled: two or three friendly pawns on the same file

Isolated: a pawn with no friendly pawns on files adjacent to it (a single-pawn island)

Hanging: Two friendly pawns abreast without friendly pawns on adjacent files

Backward: a pawn whose neighboring pawns have been pushed forward ahead of it

More pawn islands

—Level II—

Lesson Twelve

Strategy—
Pawn Weaknesses

*In this lesson, you'll learn to recognize
and exploit pawn weaknesses.*

I f pieces are the muscles of the chess position, then the pawn formation (also called pawn structure) is its skeleton. Andre Philidor, the best player of the 18th century, put it another way. He said, "Pawns are the soul of chess."

The structure of the pawns determines the character of the overall position.

There are many different kinds of weak pawns: They can be isolated, doubled, both isolated and doubled (and even isolated and tripled), backward, and hanging. But it is important to note that such pawns are not always actually weak. The pawn structure must be considered together with the location of the pieces in order to make an objective evaluation. The degree to which the pieces and pawns interact harmoniously is usually a good measure of the strength of the position.

**Gligoric—Keres
Zurich, 1953**

After 39. ... Qc4

White's defensive position looks solid, but, in reality, black has a big long-term advantage based on his better pawn structure alone. To be concrete:

1. All of the black pawns are tied together in a huge six-pawn *continent*, connected to one another. On the other hand, white's pawns are broken into three separate *islands*.

2. The pawns on d5 and f5 guarantee that black's knight will be able to use the strong square of e4. If white trades knights on that square, black will then have a *protected passed pawn*.

3. If black wins the pawn on a4, then his passed a-pawn has an open road to the queening square. Meanwhile, white's passed pawn on h3 cannot do likewise, since white's pieces do not have the power to clear the way for its advance.

These three important considerations explain well enough why black is always attacking and white is condemned to holding on. Under these conditions, sooner or later, the defense is likely to break.

The game continued: 40. Kg1 Qb3 41. Ne2 Qc2 42. g4

(desperation in a lost position!) 42. ... fxg4 43. hxg4 Rh4 44. Rc1 Qh7

Black has a decisive attack. After 45. c4 Rh3 46. Qg2 Qd3 47. cxd5 Ne4 48. dxe6 Qe3+ 49. Kf1 Rf3+, white resigned.

Doubled and tripled pawns

Doubled (and tripled) pawns are usually lacking in mobility, often lack protection from other pawns, and are thus likely to become good targets for enemy pieces. Additionally, *isolated pawns* in front of a king provide the monarch shaky protection.

Compensation for having doubled pawns often occurs as possession of the open or half-open file adjacent to the doubled pawns. And although doubled pawns often make it impossible to create your own passed pawn, they are often just as good as healthy pawns at defending squares.

Study pawn formations that are likely to occur in the openings you play!

**Smyslov—Stahlberg
Zurich, 1953**

After 18. ... gxf6

Black's real problem is not the doubled f-pawns themselves, and not the extra pawn island, but a weakened king position.

19. Qe3 Kg7 (not 19. . . Nxc4 20. Qh6 Qe7 21. Nh4 and 22. Nf5; or 19. . . Kh8 20. Qh6 Nd7 21. d5) **20. Ne5**

With the idea of going to g4. If 20. ... fxe5, then 21. Qg5+, 22. Qf6+ and 23. Re3, winning.

20. ... Qe7 21. Ng4 Rg8 22. Nh6

It's time to reap material rewards. If black moves his rook away from the attack by the knight, white has 23. Nf5+, winning the queen.

In the following position, white's doubled pawns are neither weak nor bad. To the contrary, they control key central squares. (Make a mental experiment: move the c3-pawn to b2. Isn't white's edge diminished?) And, most importantly, white is better developed.

**Botvinnik—Kan
Leningrad, 1939**

After 13. ... 0-0

Thus:

14. f4! Nd7

Opening files with 14. . . exf4 15. exf4 is obviously good for white (who is better developed).

15. f5 (This typical maneuver greatly restricts black's bishop.) **15. ... Nf6 16. Ne4! Qd8 17. Nxf6+ Qxf6 18. Be4 Rb8**

19. Rad1 b6 20. h3

20. ... Ba6

After 20. ... Bb7 , white's control of the d-file spreads to the seventh rank after 21. Rd7.

21. Bd5 b5 22. cxb5 Rxb5

Perhaps relatively better was 22. ... Bxb5 23. c4 Bc6, hoping for counter-play.

23. c4 Rb6 24. Rb1

24. ... Rd8

White has a clear advantage, for example: 24. ... Rfb8 25. Rxb6 Rxb6 (25. ... Qxb6? 26. f6) 26. Qa4

25. Rxb6 axb6 26. e4

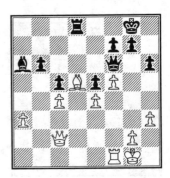

You saw this position in Lesson Eight, along with the rest of the game, when we discussed minor pieces. White is clearly better, and went on to win.

Backward pawns

Let's look at a clear-cut example of a backward pawn on a half-open file. White's position is strategically won because he can organize a successful siege of the d6-pawn.

Smyslov—Denker
Moscow, 1946

After 26. ... Qxe6

Note how white uses the d5-square for his rook, while placing the knight on another unassailable strong square, e4, from where it aids white's direct goal—assault on the d6-pawn.

27. Rd3 Rc7 28. Rcd1 Rf7 (other defensive postures also fail to hold the game) **29. Ne4 Bf8 30. Rd5**

After 30. Rd5

30. ... Qg4 31. R1d3 Be7 32. Nxd6. Smyslov won the pawn and then the endgame.

> # As the endgame draws nearer, the possibility of exploiting pawn weaknesses increases.
> # —GM Sam Palatnik

Level II, Lesson Twelve
Memory Markers!

MEMORY MARKER 1

After 1. ... Qc2

MEMORY MARKER 2

White to move

MEMORY MARKER 3

After 1. Qb6

MEMORY MARKER 4

After 1. ... Nb5

MEMORY MARKER 5

White to move

MEMORY MARKER 6

Black to move

Solutions:

MM1: 2. **Qf4! Qxa2 3. d6** (white has an excellent position: his rooks are on central files, his passed pawn is very dangerous, and his queen and knight can create numerous threats—even to the black king) **3. ... Red8 4. d7**. Despite his extra pawn, black is in big trouble—the d7-pawn ties up his pieces and creates motifs for white's tactical assault. (Spassky—Petrosian, 1969)

MM2: 1. **c4! dxc4 2. Bxc6! bxc6** (now black's pawns on a7, c6, c4 and e6 are all weak—and true targets!) **3. Qd4 Qd8 4. Bxf6 Rxf6 5. Qxc4**. And white won in a few moves. (Rubinstein—Marshall, 1912)

MM3: 1. **... d4** (with 1. Qb6, white planned to win a pawn—but he underestimated black's attack!) **2. Rxc6** (or 2. Bxc6 Qxh3, with a strong attack) **2. ... Nd5 3. Qb3** (or 3. Bxd5 Qxd5 4. f3 Rxf3!) **3. ... Qxc6 4. Bxd5 Qf6**, winning. (Antoshin—Palatnik, 1979)

MM4: 2. **Be3!** (targeting one of at least three black weaknesses.) **2. ... Rc8 3. Ra6 Nd6 4. Qe5**. The first pawn falls—now material, but not the position, becomes even. White eventually won the ending, which emerges after **4. ... Nf7 5. Qxe6 Qxe6 6. Rxe6**. (Dolmatov-Smirin, 1993)

MM5: 1. **Rd1! Bb7 2. Nf1!**. The knight will go to d5, where he'll more than compensate for various deficiencies in white's position. (Geller—Lipnitsky, 1951)

MM6: 1. **... Bf3! 2. gxf3** (even worse is 2. Nc6 Bd6 3. h3 Bxc6 4. Bxc6 Qe5 5. g3 Qxb2) **2. ... Rxd2 3. Rxd2 Qg5+**. White's kingside pawns have been seriously compromised. (Friedstein—Smyslov, 1944)

Five Reasons to Study the Endgame

1. The stronger two opponents are, the more likely a game will be decided in the endgame.

2. If you know you're prepared for the endgame, you'll feel confident about intentionally entering the endgame when you should—and you'll get good results.

3. Studying the endgame, as Capablanca explained so well (see page 166), best teaches you the capabilities of the individual pieces.

4. Much of modern chess strategy depends on being able to judge when to make the transition from the middlegame to the ending. For example, often an attacker with checkmate in mind will create weak pawns and weak squares in his own camp, thinking there's "no tomorrow." But if the defender finds a way to simplify into an ending (normally by forcing the exchange of queens), he'll win if he knows the basic principles of the endgame and how to apply them.

5. The endgame is the "last act." You could say it's "when the fat lady sings." Or, as GM Edmar Mednis put it:

> "After a bad opening, there is hope for the middle game. After a bad middle game, there is hope for the endgame. But once you are in the endgame, the moment of truth has arrived."

—Level II—

Lesson Thirteen

Introduction to the Endgame

In this lesson, you'll learn the basics of pawn endings, which serve as the foundation for all endgame play.

The endgame can be defined as a stage of the chess game with only a few pieces on the board.

The endgame is the Judgment Day of Chess, when the sins committed in the opening and middlegame are exposed and punished. Many experienced chess teachers will tell you that learning the endgame well can cause your official USCF rating to jump a full class. This encouragement is hard to deny, since many tournament games come down to an endgame, when a good endgame player will cash in the "won game" he's engineered from the opening and middlegame. On top of convert-ing won games to real points, a good endgame player will draw many "lost" positions and win many "drawn" positions. (He will even win some "lost" end-ings!)

There are three distinguish-ing characteristics that can help you to both recognize the endgame and at the same time play better when you reach one:

• Endgames favor an aggres-sive king;

•The importance of passed pawns is greatly increased in the endgame;

• *Zugzwang*—the "compulsion to move" when doing so forces a player into a worsened or even losing position—is often a factor in the endgame while almost unheard of in the other stages.

The exchange of queens usually heralds the onset of the endgame—but there are endgames with queens and even middlegames without them. A few examples:

Active king

In the game position below, white demonstrates the value of an active king.

Sveshnikov—Browne
Wijk an Zee, 1981

White to move

1. Kb4! Ne4

If 1. ... b6, then white plays 2. a4, with the threat of 3. a5.

2. Ka5 Nd6 3. Kb6 Rc6+ 4. Ka7

A triumphal march of the king! Black's b7-pawn will soon fall.

Passed Pawn

Here, white wins by creating, and then queening, a passed pawn.

White to move

The great world champion José Raúl Capablanca told us that no stage of the game reveals the true powers of the pieces as does the endgame. Those who study the endgame know the true essence of chess!

1. Rxb7 Nxb7

If 1. ... Kc8, 2. a6, winning.

2. a6

A remarkable position! Not only is the knight powerless against the rook pawn (as he so often is), but the horseman also blocks his own king's way (without a knight, the black king will stop the pawn easily):

Zugzwang

We've already seen (in Lesson 4) a number of powerful *Zugzwangs* in pawn (i.e., of course, king-and-pawn) endings. Here is another example—with pieces.

White to move

Because white always has an extra move that doesn't really change the position, namely Kg7-g8 (or Kg8-g7), it's really not important whose turn it is to move.

1. Kg8 Bg4

1. ... Be4, or any other move away from the e6-pawn, is met by 2. Nxe6, winning.

2. Ng6 Bf3 (Here, too, the knight can't be taken.) **3. Nh8 Bh5**

Black has no moves to spare, but white does.

4. Kg7

Zugzwang. The game is over.

Pawn Endings

Pawn endgames occur quite frequently—second only to rook endgames. And most endgame positions can melt down, often quite suddenly, into a pawn ending—and that tendency adds significantly to the importance of pawn endings.

Black to move draws
with 1. ... Ke6! 2. Kc4 Kd6!,
while the "aggressive"
1. ... Ke4 loses to 2. Kc4:

For the same reason, the most basic of all pawn endings—king-and-pawn versus king—are especially important. They are, in a way, the atoms of winning chess—since they are the smallest complete unit of a win. Let's study these.

King-and-pawn versus king

Put yourself in the role of defender. If the enemy pawn can be attacked and captured—you should do it, of course! Otherwise, move your king to block the pawn's progress.

And the pawn will eventually queen.

Three key king-and-pawn versus king positions

The following three iron-clad fundamental laws govern all positions with king + (non-rook) pawn vs. king.

Of the three phases of the game—opening, middlegame and endgame, the endgame has the least in common with its fellow stages in terms of principles guiding correct play.

The First Commandment of king-and-pawn endings

If the king of the stronger side cannot get in front of his pawn, the defender should be able to draw.

In the following position, again imagine yourself to be the defender.

Black to move

1. ... Kd6

Consequences of Commandment One:

As the defender, prevent the opponent's king from moving ahead of his pawn, and you'll get a draw. Thus, don't go to the side: 1. ... Kb6 allows 2. Kd5. Don't voluntarily go back:: 1. ... Kc7 2. Kc5! Kd7 3. Kd5, when

white gains even more space, and wins.

2. d5

White can't make any progress as long as black remembers the First Commandment.

2. ... Kd7

2. ... Ke7 and 2. ... Kc7 also draw, but moving—when forced to move—along the same line as your opponent's pawn builds up a good habit, as you'll see very soon.

3. Kc5 Kc7 4. d6+ Kd7 5. Kd5

The moment of truth! Here only one move, 5. ... Kd8, draws, *e.g.* 6. Ke6 Ke8

In fact, some rules good in the opening and middlegame reverse themselves in the endgame!

7. d7+ (This *check* here is a good omen for the defender.) 7. ... Kd8 8. Kd6 stalemate (or the pawn goes — also an immediate draw).

If white tries to out-maneuver you: *e.g.* 7. Ke5, then 7. ... Kd7!. Just keep your king on d7 (first choice) or on d8 (if you're forced to move back), and you'll be safe!

And—if on move 5—black erred, say with 5. ... Ke8, then 6. Ke6 Kd8 7. d7, when the pawn comes to the seventh rank *without check*. 7. ... Kc7 8. Ke7, and pawn promotes! So this is a must-know ending!

The Second Commandment of king-and-pawn endings

If the king of the stronger side is in front of his pawn, the stronger side shall win, with only one exception: if the defender's king can take the opposition, thus preventing the opponent from grabbing even more space (and therefore winning).

1. ... Kc6

The only saving move.

If 1. ... Kd6, then 2. Kd4 and white takes the opposition and wins!

2. Kd4 Kd6 (Black takes the opposition!)

If the stronger side's king gets in front of his pawn, he'll win—with one exception.

Now we have an opposition on the same line as the pawn. Black to play here loses, but white to play can't make any progress, *e.g.*, 3. Ke4 Ke6 4. Kf4 Kd5

We're back to the first key position (*First Commandment!*) and a draw.

In the following example, the defender can't reach the opposition square, and loses.

White to move

1. Ke5!

The white king is in front of his pawn, although diagonally (which counts under our *Second Commandment*).

The game may continue 1. ... Kd7 2. Kd5! White's king now is in front of his pawn; the black king is in direct *opposition* to him. As it is (most importantly) black's move, he must cede white even more territory. (Note that after 2. d5?, the white king is no longer in front of his pawn, and black should draw). 2. ... Kc7 (or 2. ... Ke7 3. Kc6) 3. Ke6 Kc8 4. Ke7

And the pawn glides to the queening square.

The stronger side should lead with the king, not with the pawn!

Check the Third Commandment for yourself!

The Third Commandment of king-and-pawn endings

If the king of the stronger side reaches the sixth rank in front (directly or diagonally) of his pawn, the stronger side always wins, regardless of who is on move.

A) White to move: 1. e6 Ke8 2. e7 (without check) winning.

B) Black to move: 1. ... Ke8 2. Ke6 taking the opposition *directly* in front of the pawn, thus forcing the black king to move aside, 2. ... Kf8 3. Kd7, followed by the inevitable pawn march.

This fundamental knowledge, these three simple *Laws*—if learned by heart and applied properly—should turn you into an expert endgamer in a majority of pawn endings you'll encounter. As a defender, you'll draw the "drawn" positions and even draw some lost ones! If you have the extra pawn, you'll win the positions you should and some you "shouldn't"!

These simple three "commandments," if learned by heart and applied properly, should turn you into an expert endgamer!

The Opposition

The term *opposition* has no magic in it. Opposition is a tool—a very powerful tool. The stronger side uses it to grab even more space, to get to some key squares; the defender uses it to stop the opponent's king.

Opposition is a special endgame situation occurring when two kings face each other, often on a file, but rarely on a rank or diagonal, with only one square between them. (In very rare cases, the kings can be separated by three squares, in the so-called "distant opposition.") In such a situation, the player *not* having to move is said to "have the opposition." Opposition is often used to put an opponent into *Zugzwang*. Opposition is a very effective tool to fight for the control of a key square.

In each of the diagrams below, the player who does *not* have to move has the opposition.

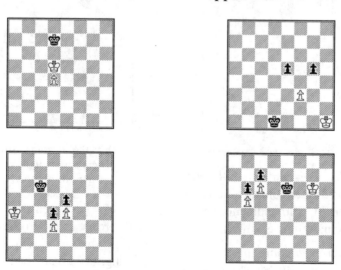

Sometimes you should even give away a pawn to get to a clearly drawn king-and-pawn ending. GM Lev Alburt liked this next position so much that he featured it on the back covers of *The Comprehensive Chess Course, Volume 1 and Volume 2*. It contains a world of instruction in only four chessmen!

Black to move wins easily.

1. ... f4! 2. Kf2 Kd3

The f3-pawn will fall soon, and no further considerations are needed (Commandment Three: The King on the Sixth ...).

But even some masters tested by Lev in the course of their first lesson, played, hastily, 1. ... Ke3? (anticipating to win after 2. Kg2 f4), only to be surprised by 2. f4!

White's pawn was doomed anyway; the only question is on which square/rank it will be captured. After 2. ... Kxf4 (or 2. ... Ke4 3. Kg2—or 3. Kf1—close to, but not on, the f2-square) 3. Kf2—*Commandment Two*, the opposition—draw.

Back to the starting position: There's more to learn from this position!

We've just seen that white's best here is 1. f4! to draw. But what if white carelessly touched his king, or perhaps badly needs to try for a win?

Both 1. Kh2 and 1. Kg2 lead to the same (lost) positions, but **1. Kh2**, moving away from pawns, can be more confusing. **1. ... f4!** (the only move that keeps the position a win for black).

If 1. ... Ke3, 2. Kg3

And here the hasty and (among those under-1600) often-played **2. ... f4+** loses for black after 3. Kg4, a *mutual Zugzwang* (whoever moves, loses) position.

Back to 1. ... f4!: Let's imagine ourselves able to hear white analyzing, as he uses "the process of elimination":

"If I stay within the first two ranks, black easily wins the f3-pawn, and the game. So, let's try 2. Kh3."

2. Kh3! Kd3!

Not 2. ... Ke3 3. Kg4, and white wins. While after a panicky retreat like 2. ... Ke5, 3. Kg4 wins the pawn and perhaps the game—unless black regains composure and recalls Commandment Two: 3. ... Ke6 4. Kxf4 Kf6!.

3. Kh4!

Also found by the process of elimination, as all other moves clearly lose.

3. ... Ke2!

This forces white to occupy a key square, g4. Black achieves the mutual *Zugzwang* position—with white to move.

After **4. Kg4 Ke3**

White to move loses

And black wins—but he had to do everything right! He had ample opportunities to go wrong, and to lose a won game!

That drawish rook pawn

The rook pawn is notoriously

drawish. Here white has *two* extra pawns:

It's an easy draw, no matter who moves first. The black king moves back and forth from h8 to g8. White can only stalemate his opponent; he can't drive black's king away to queen his pawn.

Now look at this position:

Again, it's a draw no matter who moves. Black stays on the f7- and f8-squares; if the white king ever goes to g6, then ... Kg8 follows.

The more the merrier!

As we've seen, many king + one pawn versus king positions are drawish—something like

50% are theoretical draws. Add just one pawn to each side, and the chances of the stronger side winning go up to 85%, perhaps even to 90%! Add two pawns per side, and winning chances soar to above 90%.

Let's recall Commandment One:

Easy draw: First Commandment

Now let's look at a position with two pawns against one:

White wins, no matter who moves. If 1. ... Kc5 2. e4!, and if 2. ... fxe4+, 3. Kxe4, winning. If it's white to move, 1. f4 wins: if 1. ... Kc5, 2. e4+-, and if black retreats, for example, 1. ... Ke6, 2. Kc4, taking *diagonal opposition* and soon winning the f5-pawn.

Here, with three pawns versus two, the win is even easier:

1. e4+.

White creates a passed pawn. Later, he may abandon it in order to grab black's remaining pawn—with no chance of the black king reaching the opposition square. (This method, however, may not work if your remaining pawn is a rook pawn.)

Who wins the race? (The Rule of the Square)

Many times it's necessary to know whether a king can catch an unsupported pawn breaking for its eighth rank. Of course, when the king and pawn are close to each other, you can quickly play out each move, visualizing the steps in your head—the pawn goes here, the king moves there. (That's called *calculation*.) But when the king and pawn are farther apart, such a method takes time and can lead to errors, so we need a better technique. One method is called *counting*. You simply count the number of moves the pawn needs to reach the queening square and then count how many moves the king requires. If the pawn moves first, the king will arrive in time if it requires an equal number, or fewer, moves.

There's an even simpler method by which, with a little practice, you can tell at a glance who'll win the race. It presumes that the king is unblocked from its shortest path. (If the king faces obstacles, calculation is required).

You could simply imagine an equal-sided box drawn from the pawn's current square to its promotion square. Draw the square toward the king. If the king is within the square, or on move can get into the square, he will catch the pawn. If he can't, he'll lose the race. No calculating or

The rule of thumb "The more pawns the merrier" applies to other types of endings as well, not just to king-and-pawn endgames.

counting necessary! Just be careful if the pawn is in its original position, and take into account its first-move option of leaping two squares forward!

Black to move:
The king catches the pawn.

No matter who moves,
the pawn will queen.

Practical Pawn Endgames

There are relatively few things you need to remember to be an expert pawn-endgame player: a dozen or so fundamental positions and several useful techniques. You've become familiar with *opposition*, *Zugzwang*, and *breakthrough*. Let's look at some more.

Outside Passed Pawn

A passed pawn distant from other pawns is called an *outside passed pawn* (or sometimes a *distant passed pawn*). Such a pawn is a great asset because it can be used as a decoy. The enemy king has to chase it down, or the pawn will simply queen. In this next position, despite black's prominent king, white wins—no matter who's to move.

The winning method: white pushes his passer to send the black king off to a distance. Then white's king will win both black's pawns and the game, e.g.: **1. ... Kc4 2. a4 Kb4 3. Kd3 Kxa4 4. Kd4**

And the rest is simple.

One Pawn Restraining Two

Sometimes one pawn can hold two.

White wins, whoever moves first.

We've already seen that the king on the sixth in front of his pawn wins, regardless of who's on move. On the kingside of the board, black's two pawns can't advance without allowing white's pawn to queen first. (By the way, white would win here without being on the sixth rank. See the following example.)

Sometimes one pawn can even restrain three pawns!

Here black to play wins with

1. ... h5 (or any other pawn move except for 1. ... g5??)

White to move wins with **1. g5!**. Then white "semi-stale-mates" black by moving his pawn up to a7, forcing black to move one of his pawns. White's g-pawn captures (perhaps e.p.) and, in two moves, queens and mates.

Pawns' Mutual-Aid Pact

Let's add a white queenside pawn.

The idea of 1. g5!, restraining three pawns with one on the kingside, again wins here.

But against the "natural" **1. a5?**, protecting white's pawn, black has **1. ... h5!**. White has missed his chance to play the restraining g5.

Now the position leads to an important drawish scenario: **2. gxh5** (after 2. g5 h4, white's king can't get into the h-pawn's *square* to stop it; 0-1) **2. ... gxh5 3. Kd4 h4 4. Ke3**

4. ... f5! (4. ... h3? loses to 5. Kf3, when first the h- and then the f-pawn falls.) **5. Kf3**

Neither king can capture the enemy lead pawn—and if His Majesty mistakenly captures the rear pawn, the lead pawn runs away to queen! It's a draw.

Black's king stays on b7 and a6, or b7 and c6. Even allowing the a- and b-pawns to move a bit farther, black still holds. White can stay on f3 and f4. But the kingside can get a little trickier. If, for example, 5. ... Kb7 6. Kg2 f4!

(otherwise, 7. Kh3 will win a pawn), and now white can rotate on the f3- and f2- or h3- and h2-squares. However, a further joint advance of f- and h-pawns will be lethal: 7. Kg1 (a trap!) Kc6 (any pawn move loses) 8. Kh2 f3

At this moment, only 9. Kh3 holds, while 9. Kg1 and 9. Kh1 lose to ... h3, (e.g., 9. Kh1 h3 10. Kg1

10. ... Kb7. White is in *Zugzwang*, 0-1

A protected passed pawn, a very powerful asset in an endgame, falls into the same category as discussed above. In the diagram below, black has a *protected passed pawn* on a5.

This position is a draw with best play, no matter who's to move, as white's attempt to win the b6-pawn misfires:

1. Kd5 Kh5 2. Kc6??

White's king must stay in the square of the a5-pawn; his kingside pawns aren't advanced enough to justify a march such as 2. Ke5 Kg4 3. Ke4 Kh5

4. Kf5??! (It's still not too late to remain within the square of the a5-pawn to draw.) 4. ... a4! 5. g4+ Kh6!

Luring the white king into a check; 6. Kf6 a3 7. g5+ Kh5 8. g6 a2 9. g7

9. ... a1=Q+! — and black wins.

Now let's go back to our main line (in bold) after **2. Kc6??**:

And black should win, as we'll see in the next chapter.

2. ... a4 3. Kxb6 a3 4. Kc6 a2
5. b6 a1=Q

In the endgame, rushing to advance a pawn can be a serious mistake.
Keep your elective pawn moves in reserve.
In many cases, these optional moves will allow you to take the opposition and put your opponent in Zugzwang.

Endgame principles are different!

In the opening and middlegame, we would nearly always want an extra move. In the endgame, as we've seen, losing a move is sometimes the key to winning!

Most Winnable Endgames—
The more pawns, the more winnable!

Whether your position dictates that you look for a win or a draw, you need to know when to go into an endgame and when to avoid it. Endgames can be very complex, but the good news is that there are very useful generalizations that can help to guide you in your decision.

One of the most helpful guidelines:

If you're ahead in material (and so want to win), exchange pieces, not pawns.

You want many pawns left on the board—you'll soon see why. And that makes this corollary useful if you are behind in material and fighting to draw:

If you're behind in material, exchange pawns, not pieces.

It's all very logical. If you're ahead, you want to minimize your opponent's ability to complicate and set traps with his pieces, while preserving your best chances to promote a pawn. If you're behind, you want to minimize the chances of your opponent promoting a pawn, while making things as complicated as possible by keeping pieces on the board. (Note that two knights—worth six pawns—can't force checkmate against a lonely king!)

For example, if you're looking to win, you don't want to segue into this first, already-examined position (or a position that leads directly to it), but you would jump at the second:

No matter who moves,
it's an easy draw.

White creates an outside
passed pawn and wins.

We can go even further by ranking the types of endings from easiest-to-win to hardest-to-win. As the attacker, try to transition into one of the high-percentage endgames. As a defender, look for opportunities to head into the hard-to-win endings—with bishops of opposite color as your Holy Grail!

Easiest win:
Pawn Endings

Simple rule: the more pawns, the greater the winning chances!

- K+1 vs. K: about 50% chance of winning
- K+2 vs. K+1:   about 90% chance of winning
- K+3 vs. K+2:   about 95% chance of winning

However, when there are lots of pawns, beware of blocked positions!

Next-easiest win:
Knight and Pawn Endings

In-between endgames
These include bishops of same color, bishop versus knight and queen against queen.

Least winnable endgames
The most drawish endgames contain bishops of opposite color—with an extra pawn, only about 10% of such endings are winnable! Even with two extra pawns, about 30-40% are still drawn! The second least winnable endings are rook endings.

Level II, Lesson Thirteen
Memory Markers!

MEMORY MARKER 1

Black to move

MEMORY MARKER 2

White to move

MEMORY MARKER 3

White to move

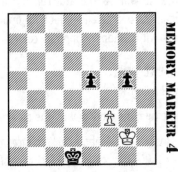

MEMORY MARKER 4

White to move

MEMORY MARKER 5

Black to move

MEMORY MARKER 6

Black to move

Solutions:

MM1: 1. ... d5+, draw.

MM2: Were black on move here, the win would be simple. White's goal, thus, is clear—to lose a tempo! **1. Kd5 Kc8** (the only move—if 1. ... Kd8 or 1. ... Kb8—2. Kd6, winning) **2. Kc4 Kd8 3. Kd4** (white loses a tempo by this "triangulation,"and black is lost) **3. ... Kc8 4. Kd5**.

MM3: **1. Ke6 Kc3 2. Kd5!**. White's king stays on the shortest route to b7 and a7, while preventing black's king from reaching c7 quickly. White wins. Instead, 2. Kd6? Kd4 3. Kc7 Ke5 4. Kb7 Kd6 5. Kxa7 Kc7, draw, happened in a real game between two masters!

MM4: **1. Kh1!**, and white holds, e.g., 1. ... Kd2 2. Kh2 Ke2 (2. ... g4 3. fxg4, draw) 3. Kg2, or 1. ... g4 2. Kg2!. Instead, for instance, 1. Kg3? loses to 1. ... Ke1! 2. Kg2 Ke2 3. Kg3 Kf1!.

MM5: 1. ... **Ka7!** (a trap: if 2. b6+?, Ka8!, draw; white has to reach to the Third Law position) **2. Kc7! Ka8 3. Kb6 Kb8**, and now 4. **Ka6!**. No more stalemates! White now wins easily.

MM6: 1. ... **h5!**, and black stands better, while other moves—say, 1. ... Kd6—lose to 2. g4, followed by 3. h4 and 4. h5.

Rook pawns are
a knightmare!

—Level II—

Lesson Fourteen

Pawns Against Pieces

In this lesson, you'll learn the key strategies in the battle of pawns versus pieces.

Many endgames come down to a piece against a pawn or multiple pawns. Of course, with a minor piece against a single pawn, the best the defender (the side with the piece) can do is draw—he should give up his minor piece whenever he can for the lone pawn, ending the game instantly. (For a very rare exception, see Memory Marker 1.) So the battle revolves around whether the side with the pawn can shepherd his pawn safely to the queening square. But when the position pits a pawn against a major piece, the situation is reversed. Because the queen or rook can give checkmate with its king's help, the side with the pawn is normally trying to find a way to draw.

Evaluations are even trickier when a piece is taking on multiple pawns. The player with the minor piece can't sacrifice it for a single one of the pawns unless he's sure he can reach one of the drawn king-and-pawn versus king endgame positions you studied in the last chapter.

In this chapter, we'll study key positions in the piece-versus-pawn struggle, devoting a section to each piece. As Capablanca predicted, you'll learn a great deal about the ability of each piece as you go along.

Pawn versus knight

Rook pawns are particularly dangerous for the knight because the horseman's moves are restricted at the edge of the board.

Here it's obvious that white must preserve his pawn if he hopes to win. Conversely, if black has a chance to capture the ambitious pawn, he does so immediately, with disregard for the fate of his knight, since the game is then instantly drawn.

The Plan

White will advance his king to c6. The knight will have to retreat to the corner. Then white's king captures the horseman by moving to b7. If black is not able to bring his king to c7 in time to stalemate the white king, black loses.

The Play

The first question for the white king is how to get to c6. Black's knight creates road-

blocks in two ways. Of course, the squares it covers are off limits to the white king. But in addition, the king must be careful not to step on those special, land-mine-squares that trigger a knight check which forks king and pawn!

These mined squares are d4 and d6, because of the knight check on b5. The invading king can choose between only two circuitous but safe side paths. One is through d3, c4 and c5 and the other—through e5, f6, e7, d7.

This last way is one move too slow:

1. Ke5 Kg2 2. Kf6 Kf3 3. Ke7 Ke4 4. Kd7 Na8 5. Kc6 Ke5 6. Kb7 Kd6 7. Kxa8 Kc7.

The black king reaches his key square in time, stalemating. But taking the "low road," in this case, gives white a win. From the starting diagram:

If we start with white's rook-pawn on the sixth rank, the knight holds.

1. Kd3! Kg2 2. Kc4 Kf3 3. Kc5 Ke4 4. Kc6 Na8 5. Kb7 Kd5

6. Kxa8 Kc6 7. Kb8, winning.

But if we start with white's rook-pawn on the sixth rank, the knight holds.

Draw

The main "trick" (more of a tool than a trick, really) shows up in the line 1. Kb6 Nd6! (the only move, but quite effective), when if 2. a7, then 2. ... Nc8+. Work out other lines on your own. Build your visualization skills by "seeing" two to four moves in your head, and then check them by moving the pieces on the board.

Here's another special posi-

tion worth knowing: In the configuration below, even with the pawn on the seventh rank, black draws no matter who moves first:

Black draws.

White can never force the knight away from the defense of the queening square. If white goes to h7, black's knight goes to e7. If white's king tries f7, the knight goes to h6. (In between, the attacked knight returns to g8, of course.) On any other white move, black can simply move his king. Once again, analyze this position in your head until you "own" the drawing method.

White can never force the knight away from the defense of the queening square. If white goes to h7, black's knight goes to e7. If white's king tries f7, the knight goes to h6. (In between, the attacked knight returns to g8, of course.) On any other white move, black can simply move his king. Once again, analyze this position in your head until you "own" the drawing method.

The closer a pawn is to the center (the f-file is close enough), the easier the knight's task. Compare the next two diagrams below:

The second diagram is the same as the first one, except all the men are moved one square to the left. White to play wins in both cases with 1. Kf7 and 1. Ke7, respectively. If it's black to move, however, he loses in the first position but can draw in the second, where the pawn is closer to the center:

First position: **1. ... Ne7+** (or 1. ... Nf6+ 2. Kf7 Ng4 3. Kg6 Ne5+ 4. Kg5 Nf7+ 5. Kh5) **2. Kf8 Ng6+ 3. Ke8**, and white wins.

Second position: **1. ... Nd7+** (1. ... Ne6+ loses) **2. Ke8** (or 2. Ke7 Ne5 3. f8=Q Ng6+) **2. ... Nf6+** and **3. ... Nh7**, draw.

Bishop versus pawns

Because the bishop can guard the square in front of a passed pawn from afar, when there is only one pawn to challenge it, the game is nearly always a draw. But when there are multiple pawns, the results vary.

In the next position, white to move wins with 1. c5, while black to move stops both pawns *on the same diagonal:*

1. ... Bd6! 2. Kb2 Kd2 3. Kb3 Kd3 etc.

The match between bishop and three connected pawns can go either way.

In the position above, it's a draw no matter who is on move, *e.g.,* 1. ... Kf5 2. Be7 or 1. ... Kh5 2. Bd6, preventing further pawn advances.

Rook versus pawns

When a major piece is on the board, as we've noted, there's even more at stake for the owner of the pawn, because now his

g material on

GLENVIEW PUBLIC LIBRARY

ATE 06/03/2017 SAT TIME 14:47

INES $13.70
OTAL $13.70
ASH $20.00
HANGE $6.30

THANK YOU
LERK 1   007623   00001

Here we see techniques usually associated with pawn endings: "losing" a tempo, *Zugzwang*, and the *opposition*. (If it were white to move here, it would be a draw.)

3. ... Ke4 4. Kc6, moving to the opposite side of the black king and soon winning.

The position below demonstrates another technique borrowed from pawn endings—shouldering the opponent's king.

White to move wins easily. The key is to cut off the opponent's king on his (in this case black's) fourth rank: **1. Rh5.** Now if a pawn moves, it will be lost—for example, **1. ... c3 2. Rh3**. Otherwise, the white king will come around and win that pawn. Black on move draws, with, say, 1. ... Kd5.

Where to go?

1. Rd2! (a tempo-losing and game-winning move) **1. ... d4 2. Rd1!** (as far from the black king as possible) **2. ... Kd5 3. Kd7**

Black to move

1. ... Ke4

Now white can't travel through d4. Black would lose with 1. ... Kf4 2. Kd4 Kf3 3. Kd3 g3 4. Rf7+.

Work out the win for white.

2. Rg7 Kf3 3. Kd4 g3 4. Kd3 g2

It's a draw. White will have to give up a rook for black's pawn.

♔♔♔♔♔

Two connected and far-advanced pawns, even supported by their king, are usually helpless against an opponent's king, which blocks access to the queening squares, plus his rook.

Black wins no matter who's to move. First, one of white's pawns is forced to move by *Zugzwang*; then pawns start to fall. Work out these simple variations for yourself, starting with white to move. We'll give you one hint—when it's black to move, just play 1. ... Rd2 and then use the same variations you worked out when it was white's turn.

Queen versus pawns

This is a very common, and thus a very important, endgame. A powerful queen usually handles even several opponent's pawns with ease. For a lonely pawn to draw, it must be able to reach its seventh rank with its king's support while the stronger side's king must be far away. But even if both conditions are met, the draw can be reached only by rook and bishop pawns. Knowing these rules, you then immediately recognize the next position as a win for white. But you must also know the technique!

White to move and win

To win, white must be able to bring his king into the fray. There is only one way to achieve this— force the black king to occupy the b1-square. Here is the winning technique.

1. Qc7+ Kd2 2. Qb6 Kc2 3. Qc5+ Kd2 4. Qd4+ Kc2 5. Qc4+

5. ... Kd2 6. Qb3!

The key move.

6. ... Kc1 7. Qc3+

Forcing **7. ... Kb1**, which allows white to bring his king just one step closer. Then a shortened version of the "dance" we've just seen will be repeated several times—until the white king comes close enough to support the checkmate, or at least win the pawn.

You should take the time now to play out the white side of this ending on your own board, making the best defensive moves for black you can find—and trying different moves when a defensive line fails. Do this until you are confident of winning this position in an over-the-board game.

Here's a sample line to get you started: 8. Kf1 (moving a step closer, as advertised!) 8. ... Ka2 9. Qc4+ Ka1 10. Qa4+ Kb1 11. Ke1 Kc1 12. Qd1#.

The same technique used against the knight pawn above works against central pawns, but does not work against rook or bishop pawns.

Black draws!

Black draws!

In both cases black continues 1. ... Ka1. In the first case, white's queen must move off the b-file to avoid stalemate, and then black moves back to b1 or b2, threatening to queen. In the second case, if white captures the pawn, it's stalemate!

♛♛♛♛♛

With the stronger side's king being close to the opponent's bishop- or rook-pawn, matters become less clear—and more interesting.

Queen versus bishop pawn on the 7th

White to play wins: **1. Kb4 Kb1** or 1. ... Ka1 2. Qd2 Kb2 3. Kc4 Kb1 4. Kb3

2. Kc3

Of course, not 2. Kb3?? c1=N+.) **2. ... c1=Q+ 3. Kb3**

Winning.

Now let's go back to the large diagram "Queen versus bishop pawn on the 7th" (page 196, at the top of the right-hand column), this time with black to play:

1. ... Ka1 (1. ... Kb1? 2. Kb4 c1=Q 3. Kb3) **2. Qd2 Kb1 3. Qd3** (or 3. Kb4 c1=Q, draw) **3. ... Kb2**

4. Qe2 Ka1! =

Level II, Lesson Fourteen
Memory Markers!

Black to move

White to move

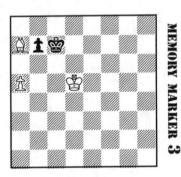

White to move

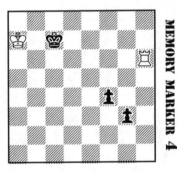

Whoever moves, wins.

White to move

White to move

Solutions:

MM1: **1. ... Kh2**, draw. (Not 1. ... h2 2. Bf3#.)

MM2: **1. Ng4** (the knight, unlike the bishop in #1, can force the pawn to move) **1. ... h2 2. Nf2**—smothered mate!

MM3: **1. Kd4!** (not 1. Kc5 b6+! or 1. Kc4 b5+!, draw) **1. ... Kc6** (1. ... b5 2. a6, with a winning position for white) **2. Bb6 Kd6 3. Kc4 Kc6 4. Kb4 Kd6 5. Kb5 Kd7 6. Kc5 Kc8 7. Ba7 Kc7 8. Kb5 Kd7 9. Bb8**, winning. (See page 223.)

MM4: White to move: **1. Rg6 and 2. Rg4**; black to move: **1. ... f3** or **1. ... g2**.

MM5: **1. Kb6!**. This wins two tempos—and the game.

MM6: **1. Qb5+** (1. Qxb6+, draw) **1. ... Kc2 2. Qc4+ Kb2 3. Qb4+ Kc2 4. Qa3! Kb1 5. Qb3+ Ka1 6. Qc2! b5 7. Qc1#**.

Some Succinct Advice on Rook and Pawn Endgames

• Block your opponent's passer with your king. Your rook is stronger and must roam free.

• It's usually better—yielding more chances to draw—to be a pawn down with active pieces, especially an active rook, than to have material equality and inferior piece play.

• As with pawn endgames, the more the merrier: four pawns versus three usually gives better winning chances than three versus two on the same flank (which is most often a draw).

• If you're a pawn ahead, try to keep pawns on both sides of the board. Also, look for imbalances. For example, being one pawn down on the queenside, but having three to one on the kingside, is more likely to win than having one pawn versus one pawn on the queenside and two versus one on the kingside.

• Use the theoretical positions you'll study in this chapter as your guides—they show you what to look for and what to avoid.

—Level II—

Lesson Fifteen

Rook Endings

Rook endings are the most common type of endgame—in this chapter, you'll learn their key theoretical concepts.

ook endings make up close to 50% of all endgames played in tournament chess! So they are definitely worth learning.

King on the eighth rank blocking the pawn

Let's start with fundamental rook+pawn vs. rook endings—a key to more complicated positions.

Draw, no matter who is to move

Here it's a draw, regardless of who's on move, as long as black passively (and correctly) keeps his rook on the eighth rank—for example: 1. Rg7+ Kh8, etc. (but not 1. ... Kf8?? 2. Kh7, and white will win).

Another easy draw

You can see that black cannot be forced out of the corner here either. But that goes *only* for knight- and rook-pawns.

With a bishop (or central) pawn, passive defense (that is, the approach of defending the back rank) fails!

"Position A":
White wins against passive defense!

Here white wins no matter who's to move. Black's rook is passive—it must protect the back rank against checkmate, and can't be moved to a more aggressive posture, such as checking the white king.

1. ... Rd8 2. Rb7 Ra8

Now, if 3. Rh7 (threatening 4. f7+ and 5. Rh8+), black counters with 3. ... Ra6, and white's best is to go back, say to b7, and

to look for the right plan—which is to win a tempo. Here is the plan:

3. Rg7+ Kh8 (3. ... Kf8 4. Rh7, threatening 5. Rh8#) **4. Rh7+**

4. ... Kg8 5. f7+ Kf8 6. Rh8+ 1:0

Let's make a change in "Position A," top left.

Draw

Here white's king is on the same side of his pawn as the enemy rook and so is exposed to immediate checks. So even with white to move, this is a draw, as black will be able to activate his rook, e.g.: 1. Kf5 (aiming for g6—on most rook moves, black plays 1. ... Ra6+, forcing white's king back; if 1. Rb6, black plays 1. ... Rc8, and white can't improve his position) 1. ... Ra1, followed by checking from behind—true active defense!

Philidor's Position

"Position B," below, represents a "generic" or matrix position that can be moved to the left or right, up or down the board. And both rooks can be placed almost anywhere (except for the black rook being on d8, or either rook being *en prise*), without affecting the outcome. It's an easy draw if black is to move.

"Position B"
Black to move draws easily

White has achieved a lot. His king and pawn are advanced to the fifth rank, and his rook limits black's king to his back rank. White threatens to bring his king (remember, generally you want to advance your king first) to the sixth rank, where it would add mating threats to black's problems, eventually chasing the defending king from his guard of the queening square.

But despite all of these advantages the position is a basic, easy building-block draw! (Rook endings are notoriously drawish!)

Philidor's Method

1. The defender prevents his opponent's king from advancing to the sixth rank. So the superior side is forced to push his pawn to use it as shelter along the rank to cross the sixth.

2. At that point the defender shifts his rook to the rear—usually all the way to the first rank—in order to give checks.

3. With the pawn on the sixth, the attacker's king can't escape the checks from behind, so he isn't able to create the mating threats needed to chase the

Philidor's Method is a drawing technique, often available for the side down a pawn in a rook-and-pawn endgame.

defending king off the queening square.

Let's do it:

1. ... Rb6 2. Rh8+ (probing) **2. ... Kd7** (not 2. ... Ke7 3. d6+, winning a tempo and the game—3. ... Rxd6 4. Rh7+) **3. Rh7+ Ke8** (or 3. ... Kd8) **4. Rc7**

4. ... Kd8 5. Rh7

White's attempt to wrestle the sixth rank fails here: 5. Rc6 Rxc6 6. dxc6

Black to move

6. ... Kc7 or 6. ... Kc8 leads to a drawn pawn ending. (Note that—in the analysis diagram—with the black king on e8, white wins).

5. ... Ra6 6. d6

All tricks exhausted, white pushes the pawn.

6. ... Ra1

Ready to check from behind —an *easy* draw now.

Back to the Philidor position—here is another one (of very many) applicable positions:

Black to move

From Lev's teaching experiences, even many tournament players wouldn't know or remember Philidor's technique (1. ... Rb6!) and would rather play **1. ... Rb5??** (pinning the pawn) **2. Kf6**

Now white is winning. The game is likely to continue: 2. ... Rb6+ 3. e6 Kd8 4. Rh8+ Kc7 5. Kf7, soon winning black's rook for a pawn.

Lucena's position

Now let's look at rook vs. rook-and-pawn positions where the defending king is pushed out of the pawn's way. Here the white king has already managed to reach the seventh rank.

White to move

Nothing can stop White from winning—if he knows the proper technique. This is another position that you should know very well—a position which can lead

by force to "Lucena's position," named after the author of the oldest existing chess book, published in 1497. Interestingly, the manuscript doesn't include this position! White can win by a technique Aaron Nimzovich later dubbed "building a bridge."

(Co-author Al Lawrence feels the popular name Nimzo gave to the procedure can be misleading if taken too literally, since there's really no form of bridge being built here at all; the key idea is really a simple sheltering technique.) White configures a straight line of rook, king and pawn on the file, escaping checks and ensuring that the pawn can "cross" to its queening square.

First white advances his pawn as fast as possible.

1. Kh7 Rh2+ 2. Kg8 Rg2 3. g7, reaching Lucena's position.

3. ... Rh2

Or 3. ... Rg3 4. Rh1 Kf6 5. Kh8 Rxg7 6. Rf1+ Kg6

7. Rg1+ with the win.

4. Re1+ Kd7

To make progress, white needs to move his king out of the way of his pawn. Moving the king immediately accomplishes nothing: 5. Kf7 Rf2+ 6. Kg6 Rg2+ 7. Kf6 Rf2+ 8. Ke5 Rg2, and the king has to come back. However ...

5. Re4!

Played to be able to provide a future shelter for the king.

5. ... Rh1 6. Kf7 Rf1+ 7. Kg6 Rg1+ 8. Kh6

The threat is 9. Re5 and 10. Rg5, building a bridge, or 9. Rh4 and 10. Kh7. That's why Black couldn't wait to check again.

8. ... Rh1+ 9. Kg5 Rg1+ 10. Rg4

The "bridge," which is really a block against checks, has been completed and white wins easily.

The defending king is cut off from the pawn.

If the weaker side's king is cut off from the pawn, the frontal attack is the most effective—and often the only —method of defense.

1. Ka4 Ra8+ 2. Kb5 Rb8+ 3. Ka5 Ra8+ 4. Kb6 Rb8+

Lucena's Position reveals a winning technique that wins, under certain circumstances, for the side a pawn up.

Black eventually drives the white king back to b3. Note that a three-square interval between the king and the attacking rook was essential for black's success.

In a starting position white can, and should, try to play for the win, but—with the best defense—black should hold: for example: 1. Rc5+ Kd6 2. Ka4 (2. Kc4 Rh8) 2. ... Ra8+

3. Kb5 (3. Ra5 Rb8 4. b5 Kc5) 3. ... Rb8+ 4. Kc4 Rh8. Or 1. Rc4 (defending the pawn) 1. ... Kd6! 2. Ka4 Kd5!

3. Rc5+ (or 3. Rc7 Kd6) 3. ... Kd6 4. Ka5 Ra8+, draw.

Winning by "Building a bridge"

1. The superior side advances his pawn to the seventh rank to reach Lucena's position.

2. He uses his rook to push his opponent's king out of the way.

3. He advances his rook to the fourth rank.

4. He moves his own king out of the way of his pawn.

5. He advances his king toward the opponent's checking rook until reaching the fifth rank.

6. He interposes his rook to block the check, completing the "bridge," allowing his pawn to queen.

However, with a pawn safely protected, the stronger side wins.

1. Ka4 Ra8+ (or 1. ... Rc8 2. Rxc8 Kxc8 3. Ka5! +-) **2. Kb5 Rb8+ 3. Ka6**

With b4-protected, this advance is possible.

3. ... Ra8+ 4. Kb7 Ra4 5. Rc7+, winning.

A rook pawn

As in pawn endings, the rook pawn is the most drawish in rook endings too. Let's examine some key positions.

Draw no matter who moves

White can make no progress, e.g., 1. Rh4 Kd7 2. Rh8 Kc7

3. Rb8 Rc2 4. Rb7+ Kc8, draw.

Here White wins—no matter who's to move:

The horizontal interval of four squares between the king and the pawn allows white's rook time to help his king out from the corner.

1. Rc2 Ke7 2. Rc8 Kd6

The trickiest defense. If 2. ... Kd7, 3. Rb8 Ra1 4. Kb7 Rb1+ 5. Ka6 Ra1+ 6. Kb6

6. ... Rb1+ 7. Kc5, and white's pawn will queen.

3. Rb8 Ra1

**4. Kb7 Rb1+ 5. Kc8 Rc1+
6. Kd8 Rh1**

7. Rb6+! Kc5 8. Rc6+!

White wins! 8. ... Kxc6
9. a8=Q+; 8. ... Kd5 9. Ra6; 8. ...
Kb5 9. Rc8.

**Rook in front of his pawn on
the seventh or sixth rank**

In the position below, the
first move is a crucial advantage:
white to move wins; black to
move draws.

White to move wins;
black to move draws.

White to move wins with a
simple 1. Rb8 (or 1. Rd8 or
1. Re8), arriving at a K+R versus
K ending — much easier to win
than K+Q versus K+R ending
(after 1. Rg8+ Kxg8 2. c8=Q+).

Black to move holds easily:
1. ... Rc1

Black pins the white rook to
the c8 square. When the white
king tries to unpin his rook with
2. Kd6, he'll be checked away
from the pawn, followed by the
same ... Rc1, e.g., 2. ... Rd1!+
3. Ke5 Rc1 4. Kd4 Rc2.

Or 4. ... Kh7. (But not 4. ...
Kg6? 5. Rg8+ or 4. ... Kf7
5. Rh7!).

Even if we add a g- or h-pawn to white in the above small diagram, the result still will be a draw. But adding an f-pawn will win—because advancing it will force the black king to move to either f6 or f7!

A practical rook endgame

To close this chapter, let's take a look at a few key moves from a classic master rook-and-pawn endgame.

Geza Maroczy—Georg Marco
1902

White to move

1. Ra2

Rook belongs behind the passed pawn (Tarrasch).

1. ... Rb3 2. a6 Rb8 3. a7 Ra8

4. Ra6!

Cutting off the black king. White wins. This is a great position to practice on your own board.

Rooks normally belong behind passed pawns—whether they're yours or your opponent's.

Summary of Chapter 15

Rook endings account for half the endgames you're likely to reach. Reviewing this chapter regularly, along with the previous two chapters, will lead to more and more endgame wins. (Remember, opening variations come and go, but winning endgame technique is always in fashion!) Next to bishops-of-opposite-color endings, rook endings are the most drawish. As in most other endings, the defending king should try to get in front of the passed pawn(s). Rooks generally belong behind passed pawns, whether the pawn is yours or your opponent's.

When rook and one pawn opposes a rook, the rook pawn is, as usual, the most likely to lead to a draw. Passive defense, where the defender's rook stays on the back rank, holding down the fortress, succeeds against knight- and rook-pawns. Philidor's position is an important one to remember, and once reached, leads to an easy draw. When Philidor's position is unreachable, the defender still has effective techniques to fight for a draw. The long-side defense can lead to a draw, if the rook has enough lateral room to operate. When the defending side's king is cut off from the queening path of the pawn, using his rook to attack frontally is often the only successful defense. On the other hand, the Lucena position is a basic winning technique in which the superior side "builds a bridge" (or at least a barricade) to shelter his king from checks and promote his pawn. Rook and two pawns usually win against the lone rook, except for the special case of rook- and bishop-pawns.

When both sides have pawns, remember that it's better to be down a pawn and have an active rook, than to be materially even and suffer the disadvantage of a passive position. When one side is up a pawn, the more pawns on the board, the more likely he is to win. In such a case the stronger side should try to keep pawns on the board in order to maximize chances of creating a passed pawn, while the defender should try to exchange as many pawns as possible, ideally making sure that all remaining pawns are on the same part of the board. After all, if a game boils down to a one-pawn advantage, with all pawns on the same side of the board, it's quite often a draw.

Surprise the Masters!

Now something even masters may not know: even with white to move in the position below, black still draws—and draws easily. (Knowledge is power—and points on a tournament table.)

White's best here is **1. Kf6**. (Black to move draws easily with Philidor's 1. ... Rb6.)

White can hope (often not in vain) for 1. ... Rb6+?? 2. e6, winning. But instead black has **1. ... Re2**, so that after 2. Rh8+ Kd7, 3. e6+ would lose a pawn. So the only way for white to start pushing his pawn is **2. Ke6**, when black plays **2. ... Kf8**.

Black's king goes to the short side of the board, leaving the long side for his rook to roam and check.

3. Rh8+

If 3. Kd6, both 3. ... Kf7 (to stop e5-e6) and 3. ... Re1 (waiting for e5-e6 to begin checks from behind) hold the draw.

3. ... Kg7 4. Re8

White is prepared to play 5. Kd7, and then to push the pawn—for example: 4. ... Re1? 5. Kd7 Kf7? 6. e6+. Instead, black should switch to side checks: **4. ... Ra2!** with an easy draw. If White tries 5. Rd8, hoping to interpose his rook, then the simplest is 5. ... Re2, falling back on the same reliable "from behind" defense.

Level II, Lesson Fifteen
Memory Markers!

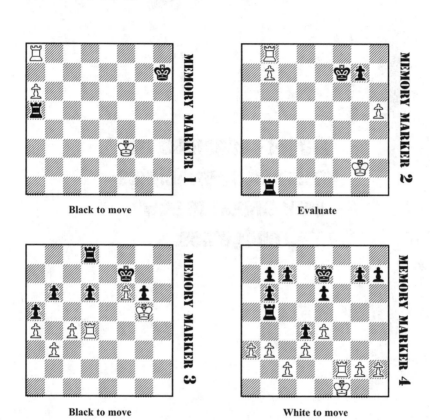

MEMORY MARKER 1

Black to move

MEMORY MARKER 2

Evaluate

MEMORY MARKER 3

Black to move

MEMORY MARKER 4

White to move

Solutions:

MM1: 1. ... **Rf5+ 2. Ke4 Rf6**, pinning the white rook to his pawn and achieving the drawish "Vancura Position."

MM2: It's a draw no matter who moves first. White's only try is **1. h6,** hoping for 1. ... gxh6 2. Rh8+-. But **1. ... Kg6** leads to a draw.

MM3: 1. ... **Re8 2. Rxd6 Re5+ 3. Kg4 Re6**, draw. (Capablanca—Vidmar, 1927)

MM4: 1. ... **Rh5! 2. h3 b5!**, fixing a weak a3-pawn. (Marshall—Tarrasch, 1905)

Knight endgames are governed by principles very similar to pawn endgames.

—Level II—

Lesson Sixteen

Knight Endgames

*In this lesson, you'll learn the key concepts
necessary to play knight endgames.*

We've so far looked carefully at some key positions in three categories of endings:

- King-and-pawn endings
- Endgames in which one player has a single piece and his opponent has one or more pawns
- Rook-and-pawn endings

In the next three chapters, we'll take a look at endgames in which there is a single piece (plus pawns) on each side.

Knight-and-pawn endings

Next to pawn endings, knight endings are the most winnable of all. Most of the principles and techniques that govern pawn endings apply to knight endings as well: the power of the outside passed pawn, *Zugzwang*, "the more the merrier" (knight + three pawns vs. knight + two pawns is a more likely win than knight + two pawns vs. knight + one pawn). But there are positions where a knight *and* pawn can't win!

White to move

After the natural-looking 1. a7, white can't win (he can only stalemate the black king, who stays on b7 and a8 squares). Instead 1. Nb4, protecting his *sixth-rank a-pawn from behind* wins easily. The knight is untouchable, so white's king can be brought to support his pawn, and together with the knight, to assure queening.

Black to move

Let's analyze together, imagining we're black. Clearly, we have to keep the white king trapped in the corner to prevent queening. So we must make one of two moves: 1. ... Kf8 or 1. ... Kf7. We know that as long as we stay on one of these two squares, the white king can't get out by himself. So it's all about the knight—if he can force us away, we lose. If he can't, we draw. So which square do we choose?

1. ... Kf8!

There's an easy mnemonic

trick that works here. When it's our move, we move to the square that is the same color that the knight is currently on. As it approaches, the knight will alternate color, and so will we.

Using this method, we guarantee that we will end up in checks like this:

Black draws: white can't keep black from shuffling from f8 to f7

Not in losing *Zugzwangs* like this:

White wins: black can't get back to f8

Knight and pawn against knight

Let's look at two masters plying their craft in the most basic knight ending. In positions with knight and pawn against knight, with the weaker side's king far away, all that's required for the stronger side to win is pushing the opponent's knight out of the way of the passed pawn. The king and knight must usually work together to achieve this goal.

**Petrov—Aronin
1950**

White's defense is difficult, as his king is far away from the path of the pawn.

1. Ne3 g3 2. Ng2 Nf5

Black limits the movements of white's knight and prepares to move his king to f3. His first big goal is to move the pawn to g2.

**3. Kc4 Ke4 4. Kc3 Kf3
5. Ne1+Ke2**

6. Ng2 (or 6. Nd3 Ke3 7. Ne1 Nh4 8. Kc2 Ke2 9. Nd3 Ng6 10. Nc1+ Ke3)

6. ... Kf1

7. Nf4 Ne7! (aiming for g6)
8. Kd2 Ng6

9. Nh3 (if 9. Ne2, then 9. ... g2 10. Ke3 Nf4!, winning)

After 10. ... Nf4 (analysis)

9. ... g2 10. Ke3

10. ... Ne5!

White resigned, as nothing can stop the black knight from reaching the f2-square. Of course, it doesn't matter if the knight "dies" on f2—its task is to deflect the white knight from guarding the queening square.

Benko—Bronstein
1949

Here the defending king is closer to the pawn (yet on its sixth rank). Besides, it's easier for a knight to handle a bishop-pawn than a knight-pawn or (heaven forbid!) a rook-pawn. In fact, here the players agreed to a draw—let's see why.

1. Ne4 Ng4 (or 1. ... Nf1 2. Ng5 f2 3. Ne4 and 4. Nxf2) **2. Kd2 Ne5**

If 2. ... Nf6, 3. Nxf6 f2 4. Ng4

4. ... f1=Q 5. Ne3+

It's easier for a knight to handle a bishop-pawn than a knight-pawn, or (heaven forbid) a rook-pawn!

3. Ke3 Nc4+

4. Kd4 Na3

Or 4. ... Nd6 5. Nxd6 f2 6. Nf5 — a familiar idea.

5. Kd3 Nb5 6. Kd2 Nd4 7. Kd3 Ne6 8. Ke3

8. ... Nc7

If 8. ... Nc5, 9. Nf2!

9. Kd3 Nd5 10. Kc2 Ne3+ 11. Kc3 Nf5 12. Kd2 Ng3

13. Nf6 f2

This leads to an immediate draw, and—believe us—we've tried our best to win! (Play it over; try other ways for black.)

14. Ng4 f1=Q 15. Ne3+, draw.

♔♔♔♔♔♔

Now let's look at the knight ending when there are many pawns on board.

Rabinovich—Belavenets 1937

White to move

White has an extra pawn on the kingside. Black has an extra pawn on the queenside. But it's easier for black to create a passed pawn because:

• Having two pawns against one is ideal for creating a passed pawn.

• It is difficult for white to create counter-chances on the kingside, because he has a less favorable pawn majority (three against two) and his pawns are poorly placed for the job. Additionally, his isolated pawn on e3 is blocked by black's knight.

• Black's pieces occupy more active positions. His king and knight dominate the center and are ready for action on either side.

Considering all of these factors, we can judge this position is much better, perhaps even winning, for black.

1. Kf1 Kc6 2. Ke2 Kd5 3. Nf5 Kc4 4. Nd4 a5 5. h4 a4 6. g4 b5

7. Kd1

Admitting defeat. But black also wins after 7. g5 b4 8. Kd1 Kd3 9. Nf5 b3.

7. ... Nf2+ 8. Kc2 Nxg4 9. Nf5 f6, white resigns.

White's position is hopeless after 10. Nd6+ Kb4 11. e4 Kc5 12. Nb7+ Kd4 13. Nd6 b4.

In knight endgames, as in pawn endings, a player with a pawn majority on one side of the board should use it to try to create a passed pawn.

Level II, Lesson Sixteen
Memory Markers!

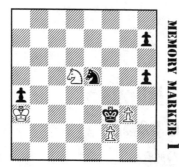

Black to move

White to move

Black to move

Black to move

Solutions:

MM1: **1. ... Ng4**, preventing 2. Nf6. Black is winning. (Schmidt—Kasparov, 1980)

MM2: **1. Ne5 Kxa3 2. Nc6**, winning.

MM3: **1. ... Nxg7 2. Nxg7 c4**, winning.

MM4: **1. ... Nd3! 2. Ke2** (or 2. Kxd3 h3 3. Ne3 Kf4 -+) **2. ... Nf4+**, with a won pawn ending.

In endings with bishops of opposite color, pawns are expendable.

—Level II—

Lesson Seventeen

Bishop Endgames

*In this lesson, you'll learn to play
bishop endgames.*

Draw

As we did with knight endings, let's start with a paradoxical position.

White can stalemate the black king, but can't drive him from his safe corner (the g8- and h8- squares). White's bishop is of the wrong color. With a dark-square bishop, an h-pawn wins easily (but an a-pawn, of course, doesn't).

Endgames involving a king and bishop against a king, bishop and one or more pawns on each side can be separated into two categories: bishops of the same color and bishops of opposite colors. The play is very different in the two groups. Let's start by examining endgames with same-color bishops.

We'll separate this chapter into two sections: same-color bishops & opposite-color bishops.

—*Bishops of the Same Color*—

"Opposition from the bottom"

Can this pawn be stopped?

Draw no matter who is on move

Note that with the black king on any other square, white (on move) wins easily. Experiment on your own. Here are two examples to get you started: with black's king on f6, white plays 1. Bg4 and 2. Bd7; with black's king on e6, white plays 1. Be8, and when black's bishop moves away, there follows 2. Bd7+ and 3. e8=Q.

♛♛♛♛♛♛

Knowledge of such fundamentals helped teenaged Bobby Fischer to draw effortlessly against a strong grandmaster in a seemingly difficult position.

Taimanov—Fischer
1960

Black to move

Black's 1. ... Kf5 looks pretty obvious, trying to get in the pawn's way. But this can't be accomplished. After 2. Kd5, b4-b5, and Kc6, White transfers his bishop to the a5-d8 diagonal, and advances his b-pawn. Black's king is shut out. So once again black needs to get vertical opposition from the "bottom."

1. ... Kf4! 2. b5 (or 2. Kd5 Ke3!)
2. ... Ke4 3. Bd4 Bc7 4. Kc5 Kd3 5. Kc6 Kc4!

6. Bb6 Bg3 7. Ba7 Bc7, draw.

♛♛♛♛♛♛

An advantage of two pawns usually wins easily, but there are exceptions, like this position:

Black to move

1. ... Bf7

White can't improve his position as his d-pawn requires constant protection. For example, 2. f5 Bg8 3. f6 (or 3. Ke3 Ke5! The only saving move. 4. Be4 Bxd5 5. Bxd5 Kxf5) 3. ... Bf7.

With many pawns on board, we often encounter a familiar nomenclature from Chapter 8—good and bad bishops. Here is an instructive example.

Black to move

A typical battle of good vs. bad (bishops). Black will lose if the white king enters the c5 or e5 squares (the latter line may require some—light—calculations). This will occur, for instance, if black plays 1. ... Bd7, as white reacts with 2. Bd3.

And black is in *Zugzwang*.

And if, from the starting position, 1. ... Bc8, white wins with 2. a4!

And the h-pawn is indefensible:

2. ... bxa4 (or 2. ... b4 3. a5) 3. Bxa4 and 4. Be8.

Same-Color Bishops: Drawing and Winning Methods

When one side has an outside (extra) passed pawn, the two main methods of defense are:

1) Creation by the weaker side of a "fortress" of pawns and pieces,

which blocks the opponent's pawns and king from advancing.

Lilienthal—Tolush
Parnu, 1957

Black can only draw,
whoever is on move.
White has built an
impenetrable fortress.

If black tries 1. ... Bg6, white plays 2. Be2, and black can make no progress.

2) The rule of the same diagonal. It is important that the defending bishop act on one diagonal while preventing the movements of the opponent's king and pawns. Defending on two diagonals could be dangerous because the opponent may create *Zugzwang* or distract or decoy on one diagonal and break through on the other.

To win, the superior side depends on:

• Effective support from his king of his passed pawn,

• Or the advance of an outside passed pawn to decoy the defender's forces so that the superior side's king can decisively penetrate and assault his opponent's now defenseless pawns.

White to move
What's white's simplest winning
plan?

Solution to diagram: White wins by using his outside passed pawn to distract the enemy king, guarding his own pawns with his bishop, and attacking and capturing the enemy pawns with his king. Therefore, he will play 1. Bc3 and, if needed, Be1, and move his king via the light squares to f7. (The immediate 1. Kd5 also wins.)

—Bishops of Opposite Color—

The most drawish of all piece-and-pawn endings are those with lone bishops traveling on opposite-color squares. The great chance of a draw in these bishops-of-opposite-color ("BOC," for short) endings is a result of the weaker side's having, in effect, an extra piece for defense. Not just one extra pawn, but two (or even three) are often not enough to win. So the stronger side should enter these endings warily, while the weaker side should welcome them!

Even great players err in these tricky endings. Pawn sacrifices, some quite surprising, are more common in these endgames than in any other, even rook-and-pawn endings, since the remaining pawns may not be dangerous. Capablanca's admonition to avoid thinking only in concrete terms, and to think also in terms of schemes applies especially to bishops-of-opposite-color endgames.

Good fortresses require bad bishops!

Capa's exhortation to have a good bishop is certainly applicable to the stronger side in a BOC ending, especially when he has connected, passed pawns. As with any "rule," there are exceptions to this one. BOC endings provide a big exception. You'll see that in many of these endings

you can cement a defensive *fortress* by putting your pawns on the same color squares as your bishop.

In fact the weaker side often draws because he can rely on a "bad" bishop and his "wrong"-color pawns! He tries to construct one of two kinds of fortresses—the king fortress or the bishop fortress. Here's an example of a *king's fortress*.

Example of a king's fortress

A king's fortress

In an impregnable king's fortress, the defending king stops the enemy's passed pawn, while the defending bishop guards his own pawns on the other side of the board and prevents the creation of new passers.

No matter who is to move, black holds easily. His king can't be forced out of his haven. When it's black's turn to move, he simply "passes" by shuffling his bishop safely along the key c1-g5 diagonal. (Note that if black's h-pawn were on h7, white to move wins with 1. h6 and 2. Be4, creating a second passed pawn.)

In a king's fortress, the defender's king blocks the passed pawn. In a bishop's fortress, the bishop blocks the pawn. The king's fortress is usually easier to hold. Let's look at a bishop's fortress.

White is ahead two pawns and even has one on the seventh rank! But black has set up the perfect bishop's fortress.

Bishop's fortress:
Draw no matter who moves first

White can't win because his opponent's king and bishop block his king and pawns—for example,

1. Kc5 Ke6 2. Kb6 Kd7 3. b5

3. ... Kc8!, draw.

Not 3. ... Bf3? because of 4. a8=Q! Bxa8 5. Ka7 Bf3 6. Kb8!

6. ... Be4 7. b6 Kc6 Ka7, winning.

A Bishop's Fortress

In a bishop fortress, the defending bishop stops the enemy's passed pawns, while the defending king guards his own pawns on the other side of the board and stands ready to assist his bishop.

The winning plan in such positions is usually to bring the king to support the passed pawn and to win the bishop for a pawn.

The defending bishop, in most cases, can't hold by itself; it requires coordination with its king. This often requires accurate play by the defender, as in the last example. Therefore, given a choice, the defender should try to block the passer with his own king, preferring a king's fortress.

It's not always a draw!

For a change of pace, let's look at some endings where the stronger side can actually manage to win!

Kotov—Botvinnik
1955

White to move

On first impression, the position is drawn: white's king covers the pawn on b3, and his own pawns are well protected by his bishop (another case where the "bad" bishop is a good defensive tool). But black has a way to infiltrate with his king, allowing him to create a second passed pawn.

1. ... g5! 2. fxg5.

If 2. hxg5, then 2. ... h4 3. Bd6 Bf5!

4. g6 Bxg6 5. Kxb3 Kg2 6. Kc3 h3 7. f5 Bxf5 8. Kd4 Be4, and black wins.

2. ... d4+!

Passed pawns in BOC endings

As usual, connected passed pawns are very strong, but only if unblocked. If the pawns are isolated, the greater the number of files between them, the greater the winning chances.

Black must preserve his b3-pawn to maintain a distant distraction, "spreading" the defense. Black is down a pawn, but his passed pawns decide the outcome of the game.

3. exd4

Or 3. Bxd4 Kg3 4. g6 Kxh4 5. Kd2 Kh3!

6. Bf6 h4 7. Ke2 Kg2, and black wins.

3. ... Kg3

Precise until the end! After the careless 3. ... Kg4?, white saves himself with 4. d5! Bxd5 5. Bf2.

4. Ba3 Kxh4 5. Kd3 Kxg5 6. Ke4 h4 7. Kf3 Bd5+

White resigns. black's king will go to c2, forcing his opponent to give up a bishop for a pawn. Note that black's bishop will protect his h-pawn and stop white's d-pawn on the same h3-c8 diagonal.

For the defender, a passed pawn is usually less valuable than a pawn well placed for the defense.

Connected Passed Pawns—
the three conditions of successful defense

Practice applying the principles for drawing in bishops-of-opposite-color endgames by analyzing the positions below, in which bishop plus two pawns are opposed by a lone bishop. You'll understand these endings more deeply in just a few well-directed moments!

In positions where king, bishop and two connected passed pawns (that are well placed, but not far advanced) oppose king and lone bishop, the defense can hold. But conditions must be just right:

• The defending bishop must restrain the "correct" pawn from advancing, ready to sacrifice itself for both pawns, drawing.

• Bishop must attack the opponent's other pawn, thus preventing the enemy king from maneuvering.

• At the same time, the bishop must always have a spare square in order to avoid *Zugzwang*.

Here white to move wins with 1. e6+. Black to move draws with 1. ... Bd7!, all according to our "Three Conditions."

If 1. ... Bc4, white will maneuver his bishop to h4 to cover the important f6 and e7 squares—important in case black's bishop counterattacks during the white king's journey to follow—and then carefully lead his king to the d6-square, followed by triumphant e5-e6.

Fortress Building & Maintenance 101

Remember, even though you can be one, two, or three pawns down in bishops-of-opposite-color endings, you may still be able to draw! Quality of the pawns is more important than quantity! Think creatively. Drawing in bishops-of-opposite-color endings when you're down material is most often accomplished by building a fortress. Here's the short course.

White to move

This position by Mark Dvoretsky illustrates in a nutshell most of the key principles of fortress building.

• Think scheme, not moves! Build, don't just play.

• A fortress, once built, requires little defense. The weaker side shuffles back and forth, staying "inside" the barricade he's created.

• Target enemy pawns, forcing them to move to a wrong-color square or be defended.

• The stronger side should advance connected passers by leading with the pawn that goes to a square the same color covered by his opponent's bishop. When he doesn't, the defender has the beginnings of a fortress. (See solution below.)

• Nuance is often more important than material.

• Both sides should respect the principle of "the same diagonal." (Don't overburden your bishop!)

Solution to the diagram: 1. c5! (clearing the diagonal!) 1. ... Bxc5 2. Bb3 (targeting the e-pawn, forcing it to the wrong color square, allows the perfect blockade) 2. ... e5 3. Be6 Kc7 4. Ke4

White has built his fortress. He now simply moves his bishop from f5 to g4 and back.

If, in the diagram at top, it's black's move, he should win.

And note that if you relocate the white c-pawn to the kingside or to d3, it's a draw, no matter who moves. For the defender, a passed pawn is usually less useful than a defensive pawn.

Level II, Lesson Seventeen
Memory Markers!

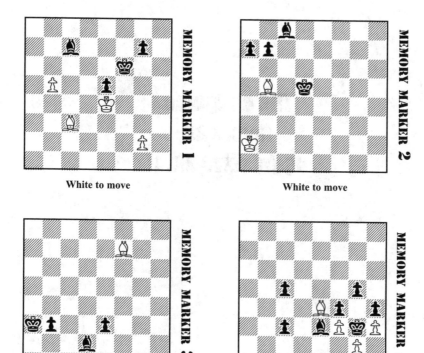

MEMORY MARKER 1

White to move

MEMORY MARKER 2

White to move

MEMORY MARKER 3

White to move

MEMORY MARKER 4

Black to move

Solutions:

MM1: **1. g4** (stronger than 1. Kd5 Kf5, with counterplay) **1. ... Ke6 2. g5 g6 3. Bb2** (black is in *Zugzwang* and is forced to play) **3. ... Bd6,** allowing **4. b6** and **5. b7**, with a winning advantage for white.

MM2: **1. Ba6!**, draw.

MM3: **1. Bg6 Kb2** (or 1. ... b2 2. Bb1=) **2. Bf7!** (targeting!) **2. ... Ka2** (or 2. ... Kc3 3. Be6) **3. Be6 Ka3 4. Bf5**, draw. (Berger—Kotlerman, 1949)

MM4: Is this fortress unbreakable too? In other words, is it a dead draw? No! **1. ... Bd4** (forcing the white bishop to move) **2. Bf5 g4** (creating another passed pawn, and winning, a variation from Makarichev—Averbach, 1973).

The endgame
favors an
aggressive king!

—Level II—

Lesson Eighteen

Endgames— The Rest

*This lesson will teach you principles
that will help you play queen endings
and endgames with mixed forces.*

To round out your understanding of the endgame, you need to learn the basics of bishop versus knight and queen versus queen.

Bishop against knight

Because bishops can zoom from one side of the board to the other, they're generally to be favored in open positions with pawns on both sides of the board. The knight is more vulnerable to *Zugzwang*. But the "Springer of Surprises" must always be watched carefully! The knight is more comfortable in endgames with all the pawns on one side of the board, and is better in close quarters, closed positions, and particularly excels against the "bad" bishop.

In the following position, white is clearly better, despite black's protected passed pawn on d5 (well-blockaded by the white knight).

**Averbakh—Lilienthal
1949**

White to move

1. g5! fxg5

If 1. ... f5, white's Nf3 and Ne5 will, at the proper moment, fully immobilize the bishop..

2. fxg5 Bc8 3. Kf4 a5 4. Ke5

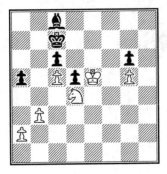

4. ... Ba6

Also loses 4. ... Bg4 5. Kf6 Bh5 6. Ne6+ Kd7 7. Nf4

5. Kf6 Bd3

White now pushes the black

king away and wins the c6-pawn:

6. Ke7 Bb1 7. a3 Be4 8. Ne6+ Kb7 9. Kd6 Bc2 10. Nd4

And 11. Nxc6, winning.

**Reti—Rubinstein
1920**

Black to move

The play is on both sides, favoring the bishop, and black's pieces are more active than their white counterparts.

1. ... Bc6 2. Ke2

2. c3 dxc3+ 3. Kxc3 Bg2

Fully restricting the knight.

2. ... Bd5 3. a3

3. ... b5 4. Nf1 a5 5. Nd2 a4 (threatening 6. ... b4) **6. Ne4+ Bxe4**, achieving a won pawn ending.

7. dxe4 b4!

8. Kd2 bxa3 9. Kc1 g5, white resigns.

Queen Endings

Queens on the nearly empty board of endgames (such as an extreme case as Q+P vs Q) can be very mobile. A defending queen poses a constant threat of drawing by means of perpetual check. Usually, checking is the best defense. In most of these cases, diagonal checks are more effective than checks on the ranks and files. When checks are not available, the defender should pin the dangerous passer to its king, and the diagonal pin is generally to be preferred.

The superior side can (1) threaten to exchange queens with

A knight shouldn't go far away from his king— unlike a bishop, a knight can be caught! And the defender should stay away from corners!

a counter check; (2) use his king to approach his passed pawn and use it for shelter from checks; (3) sometimes, paradoxically, advance his king right at the enemy queen to restrict her mobility. In endings with queens and multiple pawns, a far-advanced pawn is generally more important than the gain or loss of a pawn or even several pawns. At times the superior king can even help weave a mating net against his fellow monarch. Often, a long trip by the superior king helps achieve the transition to a favorable king-and-pawn ending.

After 4. ... Qc4+

5. Kf5 Qc2+, draw

Reshevsky—Smyslov
1970

White to move

Black enforces a perpetual check.

1. ... Qe2+ (Not 1. ... Qg6+ 2. Kh4—no more checks now!) **2. Kg5 Qg2+ 3. Kf5 Qc2+** (Yet another diagonal check.) **4. Ke6 Qc4+**

1. Qc6 Kf7

If 1. ... e3, 2. Qe8#.

2. h4 g6 3. Qc7+ Ke6 4. Qxh7 (white wins another pawn while protecting everything)

In endgames with queens and multiple pawns, a far-advanced pawn can be more important than the loss or gain of a pawn.

4. ... Qf6 5. Qh6 Qf3+ 6. Kg1, black resigns.

Because of the queen's mobility, these endgames first appear to be very complex, indeed overwhelming. However, with some experience—even after playing over these two examples—you'll improve. Meanwhile, remember that your opponent is facing very similar challenges!

Rook vs. minor pieces

Normally, without pawns, rook-versus-knight or rook-versus-bishop are drawish—but beware corners!

White wins, no matter who moves first.

White wins, no matter who moves first

Draw, no matter who moves first

In another corner:

White wins no matter who's to move, *e.g.* **1. ... Bh2 2. Rf2 Bg3** (or 2. ... Bg1 3. Rg2 Bb6 4. Rb2 Bc7

5. Rc2, and 6. Rc8, winning)

3. Rg2

3. ... Bd6 (3. ... Bf4 4. Kf5+)
4. Rd2 Be7 5. Ra2!, winning.

♕♕♕♕♕♕

Sometimes, a lonely bishop draws against a rook and a pawn!

Leading with the king, 1. Kf6, wins easily (the position is generic, the king's move being a winner if the position is moved down and/or sideways—except for the wrong-color rook-pawn, the h-pawn, where black will enjoy stalemate possibilities). But pushing the pawn, 1. f6, leads only to a draw: 1. ... Bc4 2. Kf5 Bb3 3. Kg6 Bc2+, etc. If 2. f7,

not 2. ... Bxf7 3. Kf6, when white wins, but 2. ... Kg7, draw.

Queen vs. Rook + pawn

If the defender has a pawn on his second rank, and it's not a rook-pawn, he can reach a draw by building a fortress.

Draw

Black can never be put in *Zugzwang*, able to move his rook from one safe square (f6) to another (d6) while the white king is cut off and can't even cross the sixth rank.

Endgames with several pieces often boil down to simpler ones, like those studied in this chapter. You can see some of them in our endgame work, *Just the Facts*.

Level II, Lesson Eighteen
Memory Markers!

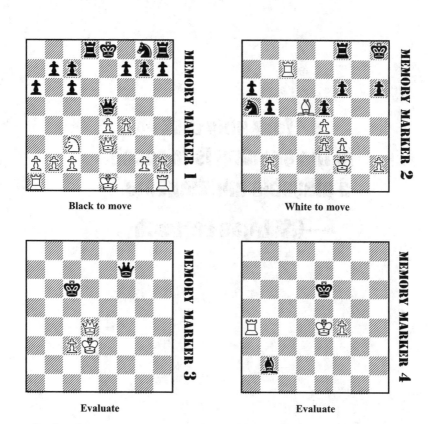

Black to move   White to move

Evaluate   Evaluate

Solutions:

MM1: 1. ... **Qe7,** with a small advantage for white, was black's best. After 1. ... Qd4?   2. Qxd4 Rxd4 3. Rd1 Rxd1+ 4. Kxd1, white is much better. The game Lublinsky—Eruchimov continued 4. ... Nf6 5. Ke2 Ke7 6. Rd1 Rd8?, going into a very difficult ending (Rybka).

MM2: 1. **b3,** preventing 1. ... Nc4. White then brought his king to h5, and won. (Botvinnik—Sorokin, 1931)

MM3: White to move wins with **1. Qc4+.** Black to move draws easily with **1. ... Qd5.** Study pawn endings!

MM4: Black is lost, no matter who is to move, e.g.: **1. Ra6+ Kf7 2. Kf5!,** with an easy win. But definitely not 1. f5+? or, after 1. Ra6+ Kf7 2. f5?— lead with the king!

**"Your only task
in the opening is to reach
a playable middlegame."**

—GM Lajos Portisch

—Level II—

Lesson Nineteen

Openings Reviewed

*This lesson provides you a review of
the different chess openings.*

What are our goals in the opening? Barring blunders from our opponents, what should we expect from a satisfactory opening?

A. Regardless of its theoretical assessment, we want a position we know how to play.

B. With white, we want a position that is at least equal; we prefer to retain some advantage, although demanding a significant advantage is usually unrealistic.

C. With black, we want an equal position, or if it is slightly worse for us, we at least want a position we know how to handle. For example, a player who emulates attacking genius Mikhail Tal may be happy with a material deficit in exchange for an attack—even if, theoretically, that attack doesn't fully compensate him.

Become a chess openings' Edison

Whatever your playing strength, nothing will improve your opening results more than some preparation—your own work in your own home over your own board. (For the serious students who have the opportunity, personal chess trainers can be a tremendous advantage, of course.)

The reasons are simple to understand. Your own ideas are the easiest to remember. Moreover, you'll play much better in a line that you've studied over your kitchen table—even if your opponent finds the best

On average, spend about 25% of your chess study time on openings.

move, and he probably won't. Chess players call new ideas in the openings *theoretical novelites*, or *TN*s for short. No one likes playing into a surprise.

Sometimes your home brewery will produce a tactical trick. Perhaps with best play your bathtub TN peters out to equality faster than the main line. But an opponent tasting it for the first time will likely get dizzy and slip.

In this chapter, we'll review all major openings. For more information on this subject, read appropriate chapters in our own *Chess Openings for White, Explained* and *Chess Openings for Black, Explained*.

There are two major (i.e., strongest and thus most popular) first moves for white: 1. e4 and 1. d4, both of which place a pawn in the center. (1. c4 and 1. Nf3 often transpose into 1. d4 lines.)

Five Reasons to Know Something About Everything in the Chess Openings

1. You need to have some information in order to make meaningful choices.

2. Transpositions (shifts from one opening to another) take place frequently.

3. Ideas from one opening can be applied to other openings.

4. Sometimes you reach a position in an opening with "colors reversed"—for example, when white plays the English   (1. c4) and black responds with 1. ... e5, the players can find themselves in a "Reversed Sicilian."

5. You can improve your overall play by practicing in different kinds of middlegame positions resulting from various openings.

Six major replies to 1. e4

**Symmetry, but white
is a tempo up and attacking.**

Caro-Kann: preparing ... d5.

**Scandinavian: cutting the
Gordian knot.**

Pirc: development first, center later.

French: preparing ... d5.

**The asymmetrical challenge
in the center.**

"1. e4—Best by test!"
—Bobby Fischer

1.e4 e5

2. Nf3 This is the most logical, and popular, move. White develops his king's knight, while attacking black's e5-pawn, and gets ready for castling. Other popular moves are 2. Nc3 (Vienna), 2. f4 (King's Gambit) and the central thrust, 2. d4.

2. ... Nc6

Black's other good responses include a counter-attack with 2. ... Nf6 (Petroff Defense) and 2. ... d6, Philidor's Defense (which cedes white space and thus, perhaps, some small but lasting edge).

After 2. ... Nc6, white has the following four choices: (a) the quiet 3. Nc3, (b) 3. d4—the Scotch Opening, (c) 3. Bc4, and (d) 3. Bb5. After 3. Bc4, the white bishop is eyeing the f7-square, which is often vulnerable after 1.e4 e5. Even on a master level, this move is quite a challenge for black, who has two major responses.

3. ... Nf6

Two Knights' Defense

Now after 4. Ng5 d5! 5. exd5, black's best is to sacrifice a pawn with 5. ... Na5, while many other responses (even the paradoxical 5. ... b5) are playable.

Or 3. ... Bc5

Giuoco Piano: the "quiet game"

White may play "pianissimo" (very quietly) with 4. d3, or go for a strong center with 4. c3, leading, after 4. ... Nf6! 5. d4 cxd4 6. cxd4 Bb4+!,

Giuoco Piano: not so "quiet"!

to a well-studied (for centuries) position. Now 7. Nc3 sacrifices a pawn (theory's verdict: equality). In our "white" book (*Chess Openings for White, Explained*), which is both a review of all openings made from white's point of view (about 80 pages) and a repertoire based on 1. e4 (about 400 pages), we recommend the solid 7. Bd2, with good chances for a small but lasting edge.

♛♛♛♛♛

Finally, we come to 3. Bb5, the Ruy Lopez, dubbed the opening of champions. Usually it leads, compared with 3. Bc4, to more "strategic" games, even if black lashes out here with the sharp   3. ... f5, the Schliemann Defense (which turns very sharp after the most ambitious 4. Nc3, but becomes relatively quiet after the restrained, and restraining, 4. d3).

Black has many other reasonable third moves: the solid, somewhat passive 3. ... d6; 3. ... Ne7 (planning to fianchetto); the immediate fianchetto, 3. ... g6;

even Bird's Defense 3. ... Nd4, moving the same piece twice.

Paradoxically, black's best (and therefore, most popular third move) in the Ruy Lopez is 3. ... a6.

Ruy Lopez:
Morphy Defense (3. ... a6)

Black's move is paradoxical because it seems that the goal of 3. Bb5 is to target black's knight, the only defender of the e5-pawn—and now black invites the capture of the knight! That's because after 4. Bxc6 dxc6 (an important moment—black captures away from the center, but opens lines for his queen and bishop) and if now 5. Nxe5?, then 5. ... Qd4 6. Nf3 Qxe4+

Ruy Lopez: after 6. ... Qxe4+

leads to a better ending for black. While another endgame, after 5. d4 exd4 6. Qxd4 Qxd4 7. Nxd4

**Ruy Lopez Exchange Variation:
after 7. Nxd4**

may even favor, very slightly, white. In both cases, black's two bishops are active and a net plus, but compare pawn structures: in the last diagram, white eventually may get a passed pawn (on the e-file), while black, with his double pawns, can't. And in the previous diagram, black's four queenside pawns can hold off their four white counterparts.

White's most common fourth move in the Ruy Lopez, 4. Ba4, may lead to a variety of well-regarded positions: 4. ... Nf6 5. 0-0

Ruy Lopez: after 5. 0-0

5. ... Nxe4, the Open Variation; 5. ... Be7 6. Re1 b5 7. Bb3 0-0 8. c3

Ruy Lopez: after 8. c3

and now 8. ... d5 is the Marshall Gambit, while the "classic" line continues 8. ... d6 9. h3 Na5 10. Bc2 c5 11. d4 Qc7—the Chigorin Variation, the blueprint of many great Ruys!

(Of course, if you, as white, have prepared to meet 3. ... a6 with 4. Bxc6, you don't need to study in depth either the Chigorin or Marshall; the same if, as black, you play the Schliemann, 3. ... f5. We call such lines "shortcuts," because they eliminate many hours of studying theory.)

In most cases, you can find a good response to the opponent's unexpeced opening move just from common sense and some calculation.

The Light-Square Strategy
Scandinavian: **1. e4 d5 2. exd5**

Scandinavian Defense

2. ... Qxd5

Also possible is 2. ... Nf6, best met by 3. d4 or the somewhat trickier 3. Bb5+ Bd7 4. Be2 Nxd5 5. d4. (Reason: wouldn't you, as black, prefer to have the light-square bishop on his home square, c8?) True, white can meet 2. ... Nf6 with 3. c4, protecting the d5-pawn, but after 3. ... c6, he should abandon it with 4. d4, transforming the opening into a Panov-Botvinnik Variation (of the Caro-Kann Defense), as the greedy 4. dxc6? Nxc6

**Scandinavian Defense:
after 4. ... Nxc6**

favors black.

With 1. ... d5 and 2. ... Qxd5, black cuts the proverbial Gordian knot, freeing his position, but at a price: after **3. Nc3**,

**Scandinavian Defense:
after 3. Nc3**

white gains a tempo, and after **3. ... Qa5** (3. ... Qd6 is a good alternative) **4. d4**, white has a bit more space—but, on the plus side for black, he develops easily. The game often continues **4. ... Nf6 5. Bc4 c6 6. Nf3 Bg4**, and here, to have any chance for an edge, white must be ready to play 7. h3, and on 7. ... Bh5, 8. g4.

Many a player—unless very well versed in this opening's theory—would hesitate to push his king-side pawns, so you, by choosing this system for black, would achieve an easy-to-play, equal (but dynamic, and not dead-drawish) position in most cases when you face 1. e4. And the line with 8. g4 isn't a winner for white—at best, it offers him some edge (±) in complex circumstances. A fall-back choice for you if someone keeps beating you with the above line: play 7. ... Bxf3!?. The theory's verdict of "±" is based on its pro-bishop bias (not valid below master level).

**Scandinavian Defense:
After 7. ... Bxf3 8. Qxf3**

Alternatively, many devotees of the Scandinavian (sometimes called the Center Counter), prefer nowadays to play their light-square bishop to f5 and then play ... e6, with a solid, Caro-Kann-like position. The same opening can often be played in different ways to suit a player's style and mood!

Black can also prepare ...d7-d5 with either 1. ... e6 (French Defense) or 1. ... c6 (Caro-Kann Defense), in order, after 2. d4 d5 and now 3. exd5, to be able to recapture on d5 with a pawn, not conceding even an inch of the center space.

French Defense

Caro-Kann Defense

Black's ... e7-e6 opens a diagonal for his dark-square bishop and thus also facilitates early castling. The negative: the light-square bishop is restricted by the e6-pawn and often winds up a bad "French" bishop, hemmed in by its own pawns. In the Caro-Kann, the light-square bishop is free and will soon move to f5 or (after white's Nf3) to g4. On the other hand, ... c7-c6 doesn't forward black's development (except for opening the diagonal for his queen, which is

In the Scandinavian Defense, after ... Bxf3, black's position is solid. He has no bad pieces—and no long variations to remember!

less important than developing the minor pieces), doesn't prepare for castling short, and in some cases—where ... c6-c5 will be called for—loses a tempo. Still, as practice shows, the Caro-Kann is at least as good as the French. Already we've seen its single but strong plus, keeping the light-square bishop "good." This benefit offsets the minuses.

When playing the French, you must be ready to defend against both of white's two main continuations, 3. Nc3 and 3. Nd2.

But one solution to both can be 3. ... dxe4.

In the Caro-Kann, after 3. Nc3 or 3. Nd2, 3. .. dxe4 is a must. In our book *Chess Openings for White, Explained*, we recommend instead 3. exd5 cxd5 4. Bd3!

Caro-Kann Defense:
Exchange Variation, after 4. Bd3!

(to stop 4. ... Bf5), favored by Bobby Fischer and further developed by our co-author of the just-mentioned book, GM Roman

Dzindzichashvili.

♕♕♕♕♕

In the Pirc Defense, black goes for a quick, harmonious development, conceding the center to white.

1. e4 d6 2. d4 Nf6 3. Nc3 g6

Pirc Defense:
after 3. ... g6

Black's idea is to play 4. ... Bg7 (ready to castle), and to address the issue of the center later, depending on white's actions. The Modern Defense, 1. ... g6, is a twin sister of the Pirc.

Alekhine Defense, **1. ... Nf6**, has the goal of provoking white pawn expansion, for example: **2. e5 Nd5 3. c4 Nb6 4. c5 Nd5 5. d4**

Alekhine's Defense:
after 5. d4

in order to challenge white's extended pawn center with **5. ... d6**, with a good game for black. Thus white's preferred line is 3. d4

Alekhine's Defense:
after 3. d4

3. ... d6 4. Nf3, or (as we recommend in *Chess Openings for White, Explained*) 4. c4 Nb6 5. exd6 cxd6!? 6. Nc3

Alekhine's Defense:
after 6. Nc3
♕♕♕♕♕♕

Last but not least—black's most popular reply to 1. e4—**1. ... c5**, the fighting Sicilian Defense.

The main line goes: **2. Nf3**.

Sicilian Defense:
after 2. Nf3

(Here you may consider playing 2. c3, Alapin's Opening.) After 2. Nf3, black has numerous replies, such as 2. ... Nc6, 2. ... d6, 2. .. e6, 2. ... g6.

They all, however, often lead to very similar pawn structures, and thus the same types of struggle. For instance, 2. ... d6 3. d4 cxd4 4. Nxd4 Nf6 (to invite the white knight to c3, thus precluding c2-c4) 5. Nc3 e6:

Sicilian Defense:
after 5. ... e6

This is the so-called Scheveningen Variation. White is better developed, and owns more space.

Black's plusses, resulting from the third-move exchange of

his bishop-pawn for white's central pawn (according to our previous "exchange rate," an advantage of one tenth of a pawn): (a) more pawns in the center, even if they are less advanced (e6 and d6 versus white's e4) and (b) play along the semi-open c-file. (See our comment to 4. ... Nf6.)

Positions like this are unbalanced, sharp and almost equal (white's edge being the smallest of *all* openings). White's most common, promising plan is to attack, while black welcomes exchanging queens—to reach what has become the proverbial black-favoring "Sicilian endgame," with no attacking threats from a now queen-less opponent, while black's plusses (recounted above) remain.

Closed Openings: 1. d4

After **1. d4 d5**, white usually attacks the center (the d5-pawn) with **2. c4,**

Queen's Gambit

the Queen's Gambit (which really isn't a gambit; it only looks like one). Now black's major choices are: (a) 2. ... dxc4 (Queen's Gambit Accepted) and two ways to protect the central pawn with a pawn: (b) 2. ... e6 (Orthodox) and (c) 2. ... c6 (Slav).

Second moves with knights, 2. ... Nc6 (Chigorin) and, especially 2. ... Nf6 (Marshall) favor white, as black doesn't get full compensation for the abandoned center (c4 for d5 pawn exchange).

2. ... dxc4 doesn't win a pawn, e.g., 3. e3 b5? 4. a4 c6? 5. axb5 cxb5?? 6. Qf3

Arbitrary Opening Nomenclature:
Openings beginning 1. e4 e5 are called "open" games. Any response to 1. e4 other than 1. e5 makes it a "semi-open" game. Any game not beginning with 1. e4 is "closed."

Why the Queen's Gambit isn't a gambit!

Black's best is to meet **3. e3** (or 3. Nf3—here, too, 3. ... b5? still doesn't hold a pawn for black) with **3. ... Nf6 4. Nf3 c5**

Queen's Gambit Accepted

challenging white's center. Often it leads to positions with white's "isolani," as in chapter 23.

Strong-point Defenses: 2. ... e6 and 2. ... c6

Orthodox Defense to Queen's Gambit

French Defense (to 1. e4)

Slav Defense to Queen's Gambit

Caro-Kann Defense (to 1. e4)

2. ... e6: Positive—helps facilitate kingside development, and early castling; it also preserves the option to play ... c7-c5 in one move. Negative: the bishop on c8 is now blocked by the e6-pawn. (Often this bishop will later be developed to b7.)

2. ... c6: Positive—keeps the c8-h3 diagonal open. Negative: it offers black none of the benefits of its cousin, 2. ... e6.

The Orthodox Defense resembles the French, while the Slav Defense resembles the Caro-Kann.

Some advice when choosing a reply to 1. d4: The Orthodox Defense doesn't require much knowledge, at least not in earlier stages. Here's a natural sample: **3. Nc3 Nf6 4. Bg5**

4. ... Nbd7 (or 4. ... Be7) **5. e3** (avoiding a trap: 5. cxd5 exd5 6. Nxd5? Nxd5 7. Bxd8 Bb4+, and black wins a piece for a pawn. Thus, our choice of tricky 4. ... Nbd7) **5. ... Be7 6. Nf3 0-0**

Even with (very) little opening knowledge, black's play is natural, and wouldn't lead him into anything worse than ±: 7. Bd3 (or 7. Rc1) b6 8. 0-0 Bb7

and later ... c7-c5.

The symmetry is not black's only option. In fact, **1. d4** nowadays is most often met by **1. ... Nf6**. Here white usually plays **2. c4**, moving that pawn out before placing his queen's knight on c3. And now ...

2. ... e6

Black develops his kingside bishop.

3. Nc3

The most principled reply, threatening to take the center with 4. e4.

3. ... Bb4

The Nimzo-Indian Defense

(Note that black could transpose into Queen's Gambit, Orthodox, with 3. ... d5.) In the diagrammed position, white has more space and often gets a bishop-pair (after eventual Bb4xNc3). Black has superior development (he's ready to castle), and can decide later if he prefers to challenge the white pawn center with his c- and d-pawns, or to attack it (for instance, in the line 4. a3 Bxc3+) with his pieces, ... Bc8-a6 and ... Nb8-c6-a5.

If white chooses 3. Nf3, black usually plays 3. ... b6, Queen's Indian, or 3. ... Bb4+, Bogolyubov. But he can also lash out with 3. ... c5, which in case of 4. d5 exd5 5. cxd5 d6

followed by ... g6, leads to Mikhail Tal's favorite Modern Benoni Defense (which can also be reached after 3. Nc3 c5 4. d5 exd5 5. exd5, although this version, which allows white to quickly advance in the center with both e2-e4 and f2-f4, is somewhat riskier for black).

In the Gruenfeld Defense, black allows white to create a strong center—in order to attack it. The game begins with:

1. d4 Nf6 2. c4 g6 3. Nc3 d5

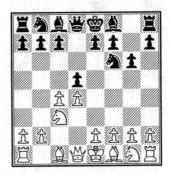

Gruenfeld Defense

The main line goes **4. cxd5 Nxd5 5. e4 Nxc3! 6. bxc3 Bg7**

(Recall, for instance, the game Gligoric—Smyslov from Chapter 10, "The Center.")

Development above all:
King's Indian Defense

As in the Pirc Defense, in the Kings Indian, black concentrates on his own good, harmonious, and fast development. He'll challenge white in the center soon.

1. d4 Nf6 2. c4 g6 3. Nc3 Bg7 4. e4 d6

White has many choices: an ambitious **5. f4 0-0 6. Nf3 c5!**

Or white could prepare for the attack on black's king with 5. f3, often followed by queenside castling (as we saw in Spassky—Evans in Lesson 7). Or white can simply develop with 5. Nf3 0-0 6. Be2 e5.

At long last, black puts a pawn in the center!

Surprisingly, even **1. ... f5—**

the Dutch Defense—can't be dismissed as "bad." A mirror image of the Sicilian, the Dutch doesn't develop a piece, doesn't bring black closer to castling—but does take under control the e4-square, which *almost* negates the negatives! For all practical purposes, 1. ... f5 is as good as the "principle-complying" 1. ... d5.

Level II, Lesson Nineteen
Memory Markers!

White to move

White to move

White to move

Black to move

Black to move

Black to move

Solutions:

MM1: White can go into Gruenfeld with 4. d4, or he can get a slightly better endgame after 4. cxd5 Nxd5 5. e4 Nxc3 6. dxc3 Qxd1+ 7. Kxd1.

MM2: 7. **h3** is the best. The tactical shot 7. Bxf7+ can be refuted by 7. ... Kxf7 8. Ne5+ Qxe5+!, and black will emerge with a piece for a pawn—winning.

MM3: 4. **Nf3**, preparing e2-e4 is the strongest, with at least a slightly better game. (If 4. ... Bf5, 5. Qb3, exploiting the weakness of the b7-square—followed by 6. Nbd2.) The direct 4. e4 Nf6 5. f3 also favors white, while after 5. Nc3 e5! 6. Nf3!, white's edge is much smaller.

MM4: Here both 2. ... e5 and 2. ... d5 are playable (just slightly worse, but sharp, clear and mostly un-researched) for black. A possible shortcut here?

MM5: 6. ... **Qd4**, and black is better—if 7. Qh5+, g6!.

MM6: Black equalized here with a thematic **4. ... Nxe4! 5. Nxe4!** (5. Bxf7+?! Kxf7 6. Nxe4 d5 favors black) **5. ... d5 6. Bd3 dxe4 7. Bxe4 Bd6**.

—Level III—
Getting Tournament Tough

By now you've acquired a lot of essential chess knowledge—enough to make you a strong, successful tournament player. In the remaining lessons, you'll learn how to handle some truly advanced but very practical concepts—the two bishops, the isolani, and the queen versus two rooks or three minor pieces. In addition, we'll provide you with advice on how you can effectively work on your own—choosing openings, picking the right books to learn from, even managing time during the game. You're now on your way to becoming a true chess Expert!

—Level III—

Lesson Twenty

The Bishop Pair

*In this lesson, you'll learn how to use
the bishop pair to your advantage.*

The bishop is a "long-distance" piece. A lone bishop, however, is able to control only the squares of one color. But when you can rely on the strength of two bishops, then both light and dark squares can be under your control.

Typical advantages resulting from the two bishops

• The opponent's bishop and knight (or two knights) are uncoordinated.

• The two bishops exert concentrated influence over the decisive section of the board—and sometimes over the entire board.

• The enemy's pieces, due to the limited mobility of the knight, arrive late to the important action. (This advantage can sometimes be transformed into cutting off one of the enemy's minor pieces, usually a knight.)

• At the moment of your choice, one of your bishops can be exchanged for the opponent's knight, while it is much more difficult for your opponent, at any given moment, to exchange his knight for your bishop.

However, the two bishops are not always dangerous. When the position is blocked or where there are no open diagonals for the bishop to use, the knights turn out to be stronger.

Bogolyubov—Janowsky
New York, 1924

After white's 23rd move

Black sacrificed a pawn to reach this position—and he was right to do so! The position is very sharp and unclear; it is perhaps approximately equal, but, even on a GM level, it's easier to attack than to defend!

23. ... Bf6 24. Qh5 Ba4!?
25. Re1 Qd6 26. h3 Bc2!

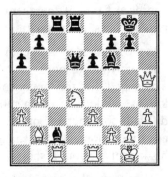

27. Qf3 b5 28. Qe2 Ba4 29. Qf3
Rc4 30. Ba1 Rdc8 (30. ... e5 deserves attention)

31. Rb1

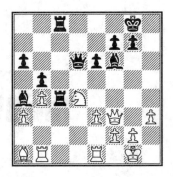

White can't protect his light squares—his pawns are located on dark squares, and he does not have a light-squared bishop.

31. ... e5

Trying to dislocate the white knight.

32. Ne2 (stronger was 32. Qg3, and then 33. Nf3, with a sharp, unclear game) **32. ... Bc2**
33. Rbc1 Be4 34. Qg4 Bb7

The bishop has taken up a threatening position.

35. Rxc4

Here white's best line was 35. Red1.

35. ... Rxc4 36. f4

Protecting the queen—but at a price.

36. ... Qd2 37. Qg3 Re4

Hours of handling a super-sharp position and time pressure may have combined to blind the players. Here black missed a killer: 37. ... exf4! 38. Nxf4 (38. exf4 Bxa1 39. Rxa1 Qxe2) 38. ... Rc1 39. Bxf6 Qxe1+.

38. Bc3 Qd5 39. Bxe5?

39. Qf3 would keep the game going.

And now both 39. ... Rxe3 (game) or 39. ... Rxe5 40. fxe5 Bh4 wins easily for black. This contest, like most games, was far from flawless—but exciting and instructive.

♛♛♛♛♛♛

The following endgame is a quintessential Steinitz: building up small plusses and, of course, the bishop pair's power!

English—Steinitz
London, 1883

Black to move

1. ... c5

Denying the knight the d4-square.

2. Bg5 f6

This isn't a weakening move, as black's bishops control squares of both colors, and his pawns remain mobile.

3. Bf4 Kf7 4. f3 g5 5. Rxd8 Rxd8 6. Be3

6. ... h6

Black prepares to build a new pawn chain (h6-g5-f4) further "caging" the white bishop.

7. Re1 f5 8. f4

A concession—in order to stop f5-f4.

8. ... Bf6 9. g3 a5

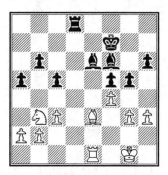

A typical anti-knight thrust of the rook pawn. The threat is (a5)-a4-a3. Thus:

10. Nc1 a4 11. a3 Bc4 12. Kf2

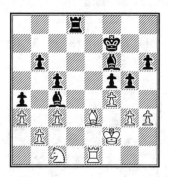

12. ... gxf4

A technique to remember for such positions: in a proper moment—of his choice—the side with two bishops initiates an exchange (here an exchange of bishops), segueing into a won ending.

13. Bxf4 Bg5 14. Bxg5

If 14. Ke3, Kf6.

14. ... hxg5 15. Ke3 Kf6 16. h4 gxh4 17. gxh4

17. ... Re8+

Simplifying into a won pawn ending (yes, pawn ending, as after the knight's move, it will be exchanged).

18. Kf2 Rxe1 19. Kxe1 Ke5 20. Ne2 Bxe2 21. Kxe2 Kf4

Of course, Steinitz foresaw and calculated far enough (on move 16, perhaps) to see that, despite white's outside passed pawn, black's active king secures a black win!

22. c4 Kg4 23. Ke3 f4+!

Of course, not 23. ... Kxh4??
24. Kf4+-.

24. Ke4 f3 25. Ke3 Kg3, White resigned.

How to play against two bishops

We now know that the bishops are very dangerous if they have open diagonals. That's why the basic method of play against two bishops is (1) to limit their activity by creating pawn blockades, (2) to conquer support squares for the knight(s) and (3) to exchange the most dangerous of the opponent's bishops.

Psakhis—Tukmakov
Rostov-on-Don, 1993

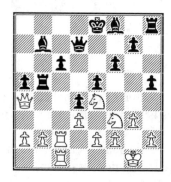

White to move

The b7-bishop is blocked by its own pawn on c6. The white knights are well placed in the center. Let's see how they make use of weaknesses in the enemy camp.

20. Nh4! Rh6 21. b3 Qd5

It was probably better to play

21. ... g5 and 22. ... Rg6.

22. Qc4!

White is correct in offering the exchange of queens.

22. ... Kd7

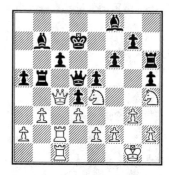

23. Qxd5+ Rxd5 24. Nc5+

An unpleasant shot. Now there will be no talk about the "advantage of the two bishops" since at least one of them will be exchanged.

24. ... Bxc5 25. Rxc5 Rh8
26. Nf3!

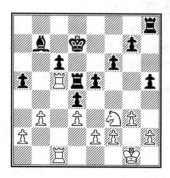

The game has been simplified into an ending where the white knight is stronger than the opponent's bishop. Now it is very important to use the knight's abilities to the maximum, so white returns it to the center.

26. ... Rb8

On 26. ... Kd6, 27. Nd2! will follow, and if 27. ... f5, then 28. Rxa5. Forks are everywhere!

27. Nd2 Ba8 28. R5c4 Kc7 29. Ne4 Rb4

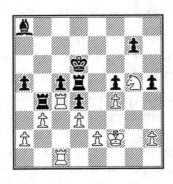

34. ... Rb7 35. Ne4+ fxe4 36. dxe4 Rf7 37. exd5 Rxf4+ 38. Ke1 Bxd5 39. Rxc5

30. Kg2!

White is activating the king. Its ideal post would be h4.

30. ... f5 31. Ng5 Kd6 32. f4 exf4 33. gxf4 c5?!

This pseudo-active move loses material. White is ready to deliver a crushing blow.

34. Kf2

White's positional advantage has been transformed into a winning material advantage (an extra Exchange here is enough to secure a quick, easy win).

39. ... Rg4 40. Rxa5 Rg1+ 41. Kd2, and black resigns.

Level III, Lesson Twenty
Memory Markers!

After 1. f5

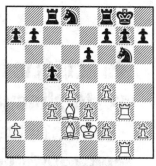

After 1. Rag1

Solutions:

MM1: **1. ... Rc8!** (of course not 1. ... Bxd3 2. Rd2) **2. Bd1** (other choices are no better: either abandoning the c-file, or after 2. Rxc8 Bxc8 3. g4 Be3, cutting off the knight, as in the game) **2. ... Rxc2 3. Bxc2 Ke5 4. g4** (see diagram at right) **4. ... Be3** (cutting off the knight, as promised) **5. Kf3 Kd4 6. Bb3 Bb7** (preventing 7. Bxd5—and winning soon. (Tarrasch—Rubinstein, 1922)

MM2: **1. ... c4! 2. Bc2 f5!**. The bishops are restricted, while the knights will soon occupy strong central squares. (White's error was 1. Rag1, betting on an unrealistic attack. Instead, 1. f5 would have led to an edge for white.) **3. Bc1 Rf7 4. Ba3** (see diagram at right) **4. ... Rc6 5. Bc5 Ra6 6. a4 Nc6 7. Rb1 Rd7 8. Rgg1 Nge7** and **9. ... Nd5**. (Em. Lasker—Chigorin, 1895)

An ability to foresee, even to create, situations in which the values of the pieces differ substantially from the norm is a sign of a true chess master.

"All chess pieces possess two values: absolute and relative. In simple positions, the absolute value is foremost; the more complicated the position, the more important a relative value becomes."
—Rudolf Spielmann in *The Theory of Sacrifice*

—Level III—

Lesson Twenty-One

The Struggle Between Differently Composed Forces

*In this lesson, you'll learn that reaching a conclusion
about the relative value of the pieces on the board
is not a matter of simple arithmetic!*

As we've seen, the chess-board gets very interesting—and very challenging—when armies made up of unlike pieces oppose each other. Let's take a look at some model play involving these "mixed bags."

Two rhinos vs. an elephant

We'll begin by examining a fairly frequent set of unlike adversaries—the queen versus two rooks.

Is the queen + pawn = two rooks equation true? It is—in many *late* endings, with no other pieces left. Such as:

The a4-pawn is a goner, and, after its disappearance, black's f-pawn becomes a target. Black can't simply sit and wait; he must do something—try to exchange some kingside pawns, especially, in order to expose the white king to checks—to make a draw.

Some sample lines: 1. ... Qe4! 2. Rf4 Qc2 3. Raxa4 g5! 4. Rac4 Qa2 5. Ra4 Qc2 6. Rac4, and white has to repeat the position, since otherwise f2 will fall with check, and black would be better. (If white plays 3. h4, black's drawing idea is similar: 3. ... h6 4. Raxa4 g5.)

♛♛♛♛♛♛

But with many pieces (and pawns) onboard—in the openings and many middlegames—the queen is most frequently equal, and sometimes stronger, than two rooks.

Bronstein—Kotov
Budapest, 1950

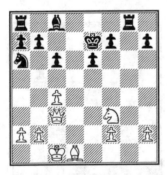

After 16. ... Ke7

The queen is especially powerful when:

a) the opposing king can be threatened with checkmates (of course);

b) the opposing king is exposed to checks (checks aren't lethal, but they allow the queen to roam the entire board, *with tempos)*;

c) the opponent's position offers loose pieces or pawns to attack and double attack.

In the position above, white is behind in material—he has a queen versus two rooks + a pawn, but white is ahead in development. He must attack, and David Bronstein, circa 1950, didn't need any special inducement to attack!

17. Ne5 Bd7

What if 17. ... f6, driving the knight back? Well, the knight will refuse! 18. Qh3! (a nice in-between move),

and white is winning (18. ... fxe5 19. Qxh7+ Kf8 20. Bh5).

A queen plus a supported knight is a superb checkmating machine!

18. Qa3+

As promised, a meaningful check.

18. ... c5 19. Qf3

And now a promised double-attack (even if without check). Just a few moves, and white is getting ahead in material, while continuing his attack.

19. ... Rad8 20. Qxf7+

20. Qxb7 also wins, but Bronstein goes for the jugular, producing tactical fireworks.

20. ... Kd6 21. Qf4 Rdf8 22. Nf7++ Ke7 23. Bh5

A queen plus a supported knight is a superb checkmating machine!

The game continued: 23. ... Bc6 24. Qd6+ Kf6 25. Nh6

25. ... Rg1+ 26. Kd2

Black's forces are disorganized and can neither launch a true counterattack nor organize a true defense.

26. ... Kg7 27. Ng4 Rxg4

To break up the mating mechanism, black is forced to give up an Exchange.

28. Qe7+ (white's play remains precise) 28. ... Kh6 29. Bxg4 Rxf2+ 30. Ke3 Rf1 31. h4.

A new mating machine has been put together!

31. ... Kg6

Avoiding 32. Qg5#? Or, rather, delaying it for one move.

32. Bh5+, and mate next move.

♛♛♛♛♛

The queen is equal or slightly stronger than the rook, bishop and pawn together, and slightly stronger than the rook, knight and pawn as a team. So, material in the following position is even. But, unlike the previous game, the queen and her side have no loose targets, and no checks to quickly relocate the queen.

Hort—Alburt
Decin, 1977

After 24. ... Rxb4

25. Nf3 Bg7

Here the queen is prey, not predator!

26. Qh3

Also bad is 26. Qe3 Re4 27. Qd2 Bc4, with the winning threat of 28. ... Ra2, or 26. Qd2 Bc4 with the same threat, when white's position is hopeless. And 26. Qg5 (gaining a tempo by the attack on the e7-pawn) is no better because of 26. ... Re4, attacking the e2 pawn and protecting the e7-pawn. If white now plays 27. e3 or 27. Be3, the reply 27. ... h6, or the equally effective 27. ... f6, spells disaster. This is a rare case of a queen having apparently free play in the middle of the board, but actually being restricted by the opponent's army—and caught. Now the queen has been forced into a very unpleasant position.

26. ... Be6 27. Qf1

Protecting the pawn on e2.

27. ... Bc4 28. Kg2

Preparing to protect the e2-pawn with the knight.

28. ... Ra1 29. Ng1

An astonishing smothering of the queen: She has no moves

and is completely surrounded by her own pieces. It's the culmination of black's strategy. White's other pieces are also poorly placed, especially when compared with the effectiveness of their counterparts. Now it is not difficult for black to find a win.

29. ... Rbb1 30. Kh3

To make space for the queen! However, such moves are made from desperation and cannot really save the game.

30. ... h5

To answer 31. Qg2 with 31. ... Be6+ 32. Kh4 Rxc1, and then ... Bf6 mate.

31. f4

Making some room, but creating a decisive weakness on e3.

31. ... Be6+ 32. Kg2 Nd5

With the threat of 33. ... Rxc1 and 34. ... Ne3+.

33. Kf3 Bc3 34. Rd1 Bb2

White resigned.

Queen versus minor trio

A simple evaluation chart shows: Queen = 9 pawns = 3 minor pieces.

If a queen were equal to ten pawns, it should dominate the trio. In reality, however, three minors are more likely than not to be stronger than a queen! (For which we can guess three reasons: 1) determining the value of pieces isn't simple arithmetic; and 2) a minor piece, except in the late endgame, is stronger than three pawns; 3) two bishops, when present, increase the power of the trio by, on average, half a pawn).

Bondarevsky—Karasev
Kharkov, 1963

Black to move

After **1. ... exf4?!**, white should "blunder his queen" with **2. Qxd4 Nxe4** and now **3. Qxg7+ Kxg7 4. Nxe4**

Black has a queen and two pawns for three minor pieces, but he'd be lucky to withstand white's attack and to hold to a draw.

Overestimating the value of the queen

Many chess players subconsciously treat a queen as if her relative value is almost unlimited—and act accordingly. This often leads to mistakes and to missed opportunities.

Leonards (1767)—Guzman (1442)

After 20. ... d4 21. exd4 Rxd4

In parenthesis are USCF ratings. The entire game was (quite ably) annotated by Edward Guzman, the eventual winner, who put an "exclam" to his last move and clearly thought his position was better—an opinion probably shared by his higher-rated opponent.

Mr. Guzman gives 21. ... Rxd4 an "!"—with the comment, "Of course, white can't take or else he will lose material. Main variation: 22. cxd4 Nce4+

White to move

23. Nxe4 Qh4+ 24. Ng3 Rxc2 and wins!"

But let's look at the analysis diagram we've placed above.

There 23. Qxe4! leaves white with extra material after 23. ... Nxe4+ 24. Nxe4.

White has a rook and two minor pieces for a queen: even after black wins a pawn, perhaps even two (which he should), material and the position would be approximately equal.

But, apparently, both players didn't even consider the idea of trading the white queen for anything but its enemy counterpart!

Two Rooks vs.
Three Minor Pieces

Let's make yet another attempt to measure the value of chess pieces by simple arithmetic.

In Lesson One, we suggested that:

• 3 minors each = 3 pawns, for a total of 9 points

• 2 rooks = 5 pawns each, for a total of 10.

But actually three minors are at least as good as two rooks. Should we award each a value of 3.5 pawns? But then—what about the value of the Exchange—which would become one and a half pawns rather than the more usual valuation, two pawns?

Let's look at a grandmaster study of these pieces in action.

Capablanca—Alekhine
Nottingham, 1936

After 1. ... Qf6

White's extra pawn is doubled and isolated; there is no potential for either side to create a passed pawn. Black's last move offers to exchange queens—which usually benefits the side with rook(s) versus minor piece(s).

2. Qxf6

But Capablanca welcomes the ending, seeing that black won't be able to activate his rooks. In fact, he foresaw how to win. The game continued 2. ... gxf6 3. Nd2 f5 4. b5

4. ... a5 5. Nf1 Kf7 6. Ng3 Kg6 7. Bf3 Re7 8. Kf1 Kf6 9. Bd2 Kg6 10. a4

Here black resigned. Capablanca later demonstrated the following winning plan: his h-pawn is pushed to h5, his bishops are placed on c3 and h3. Meanwhile, black plays h7-h6 (to get an escape square for his king, after h4-h5+, on h7), keeps his rooks on f7 and f8 to protect the f5-pawn, and moves his king from h7 to g8 and back. At that time, white moves his king to f3, then his knight (via f1 and e3) to d5, and black pawns start to fall.

The winning position foreseen many moves ahead by Capa!

Rook plus pawn(s) versus two minor pieces

We've seen that the relative value of various mixtures of pieces can change. What's more, the relative value of the pieces does change according to the stage the game is in.

Let's look at some generally accepted values of piece "bundles" in different stages of the game. We use the piece abbreviations, so it looks a bit like algebra. (Recall that ">" means "more than," while "<" means "less than," and that "≤" means "less than or equal to," while "≥" means "more than or equal to.")

In the opening and middlegame:
$$R+2p < 2 \text{ Bs};$$
$$R+2p \leq B+N$$
$$R+2p \geq 2 \text{ Ns}$$

In the endgame,
$$R+2p = 2B$$
$$R+1p \leq B+N$$
$$R+1p \geq 2 \text{ Ns}$$

In short, exchanging queens—for the side with pieces—equals losing a pawn. (The exchange of queens normally marks the beginning of the endgame, and the increasing value of rooks and pawns.) Exchanging his only "unique" rook for the opponent's "redundant" rook makes things even worse—unless the opponent's rooks work very well together, such as Nimzo's rooks on the seventh rank ("the blind pigs" which devour everything)!

An Exchange is equal (on average) to two pawns.

Piece versus three pawns

In the middlegame a piece is usually better than three pawns, unless the side with pawns a) has the initiative, b) owns pawns that are far advanced and severely hinder the activity of the oppo-

Determining the value of pieces isn't simple arithmetic. The actual relative values change constantly, as the position changes.

nent's pieces, or c) are well-placed connected central pawns.

Again, for the side with pawns—try to keep your pawn majority together. For example, three-versus-three on the queenside and four-versus-one on the kingside is better than three-ver-sus-two and four-versus-two. The extra pawn mass must be prominent to fully compensate for a piece! In the endgame, of course, the value of pawns grows—as we already have seen, from instances in Chapter 14.

Level III, Lesson Twenty-One
Memory Markers!

MEMORY MARKER 1

Black to move

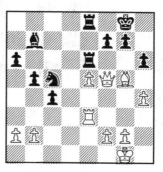

MEMORY MARKER 2

White to move

Solutions:

MM1: **1. ... Rxd3! 2. Nxd3 Bb5 3. Rd2 Nxe4 4. Rd1 Nc3 5. Rd2 Nxd5**, with advantage for black. (Gligoric—Keres, 1964)

MM2: **1. Bf6!** (attack the king!) **1. ... g6** (or 1. ... gxf6 2. exf6; 1. ... Nd7 2. Rg3) **2. Qf4 Kh7 3. Bg5! f5 4. exf6**, winning. (Euwe—Gruenfeld, 1936)

**Often the best way to
handle a sacrifice as a
defender is to return,
at the right moment,
your opponent's gift—
all or part of it.**

—Level III—

Lesson Twenty-Two

Compensation for Sacrificed Material

The compensation for a sacrifice can be tactical or strategic, sufficient or insufficient.

A sacrifice intentionally gives up material in the hopes of some future gain. In that respect, a sacrifice is always a combination. So, first, let's make sure to understand what a sacrifice is and what it is not. The diagram below shows a move that is *not* a sacrifice.

1. Nf7+ and 2. Nxd6, winning

The knight-fork move above is a simple tactic (double-attack), but not a combination.

Contrast that with the situation below.

1. Qh8+!

This sacrifice of the queen starts a real *combination*, which makes use of the tactic of double attack: 1. ... Kxh8 2. Nxf7+, winning.

The sacrifice above isn't, however, a true sacrifice, as white knew that in two moves he'd get the sacrificed material (the queen) back, and with dividends (the bishop). Sometimes we call such a combination a *sham sacrifice*. (Don't misunderstand—such a combination can still be the best line!)

Examine these two positions:

After 1. e4 c5 2. d4 cxd4
3. c3 dxc3 4. Nxc3

After 1. d4 Nf6 2. c4 c5 3. d5 b5 4. cxb5
a6 5. bxa6 g6 6. Nc3 Bxa6 7. Nf3 d6

In the first position—a Smith-Morra Gambit (against the Sicilian Defense), white's compensation for a pawn is mostly *dynamic*, residing in the relative *activity* of his pieces: he is ahead approximately three tempos in development, considered to be a full compensation for a pawn in the opening. But as the black king is quite well guarded and safe, a successful direct assault isn't immediately in the offing. White's most likely plan will be

to translate his dynamic edge into something permanent—like a weak d6-pawn for black (after e7-e6) and a strong d5-square for white—after e7-e6-e5.

In the second—a Benko Gambit position, black also enjoys somewhat superior development, but here his advantages—his compensation (for a pawn) is mostly positional and *static*, residing in the *position and pawn structure* of his army. His pawns are all in one huge continent, and his rooks will work on the semi-open a- and b-files, cooperating well with his g7-bishop. Still, even these examples show that static and dynamic advantages rarely occur in a pure form; usually there is some mix of both.

But note that in neither case can the side which has sacrificed a pawn realistically hope to get it back—certainly not by a forced maneuver, and most likely not soon.

It's easier to attack than to defend!

This maxim is certainly true for those below grandmaster level (and even for many grandmasters). It becomes even more pronounced in short time controls that are popular today. Thus the popularity of *Gambits*, i.e., openings in which one side sacrifices a pawn, whether they are solid gambits like the Benko or Smith-Morra, or dubious pawn-gifts like the Englund Gambit—1. d4 e5.

You should learn to evaluate and to employ (or when required, to withstand) sacrifices in your play. Being surprising, they are even more shocking to opponents than well-studied gambits!

Let's look at some examples.

**Hort—Keres
Oberhausen, 1951**

After 1. ... Rd2

The two well-advanced black pawns are stronger than white's queen! Black won after 2. Rxb2 cxb2 3. Qb3 Rd8 4. Qc2 Rb8 5. Qb1 g6 6. g4!

6. ... Ra8 7. Kg2 Ra1 8. Qc2 b1=Q 9. Qc7+ (white's counter-attack is his best, but not sufficient, chance) 9. ... Bg7 10. Bd4 Qf1+ 11. Kg3 f4+ 12. Kxf4 Qc1+ 0:1

Later the defense 2. Qb5 was suggested. Still, after 2. ... c2 3. Qf1 Rd5,

black has excellent winning chances.

♛ ♛ ♛ ♛ ♛ ♛

In the following position, white sacrifices the Exchange for mostly *strategic* compensation.

QN2 is the worst square for the knight!

Kasparov—Shirov
1994

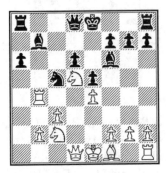

White to move

1. Rxb7!!

White exchanges his clumsily-placed rook for black's best minor piece, while forcing the second-best minor piece, the c5-knight, to the worst square possible.

1. ... Nxb7 2. b4!

The knight is caged. The game continued:

2. ... Bg5 3. Na3 0-0 4. Nc4 a5

The rule is "passed pawns must be pushed," but not here! Above all, the knight must be contained.

5. Bd3 axb4 6. cxb4 Qb8 7. h4!

Choose your diagonal, please!
7. ... Bh6

(7. ... Bd8 will cut off the f8-rook and take the only available retreat square from the b7-knight). Now, however, the e7-square becomes available for the white knight.

8. Ncb6 Ra2 9. 0-0 Rd2 10. Qf3 Qa7 11. Bb5! Dominance!

(Better than the immediate 11. Nd7, allowing 11. ... Ra8, as played in the game.) If, after 11. Bb5!, 11. ... Nd8 12. Nd7 Ne6 13. Ne7+ Kh8 14. Nxf8 Qxe7 15. Nxe6, with a clear advantage for white. And after 11. ... Rd8 12. Ne7+ Kf8 13. Nbd5 Ra8 14. Bc6,

black is practically paralyzed.

Note that many (14, to be precise) moves after 1. Rxb7 in our starting position, the black knight is still haplessly lingering on "QN2," as the old notation put it.

How far ahead should white have seen before sacrificing? Strictly speaking, one move only: 1. ... Nxb7 2. b4. Perhaps calculating a few short sample lines might be recommended, assuming white had plenty of time—but in rapid (30 minutes for each player for the game) or blitz (five minutes for each for the whole game), the sacrifice should take less than a minute!

♛♛♛♛♛

The next sacrifice, on the other hand, is 99% *tactical*!

Alekhine-Yunge
Prague, 1942

White to move

For a pawn, white has some compensation: somewhat better development, strong light-square bishop, control over the a-file, and pressure along the c-file. The

question: What to do before most of this *dynamic* advantage evaporates?

Sacrificing a second pawn (for a check) with 1. b4 doesn't look reassuring after 1. ... Bxb4 2. Bc6+ Ke7. And after 1. Bg5 the simple 1. ... 0-0 promises black an easy equality. Thus, **1. Ra6** — an Exchange sacrifice aimed at keeping the black king in the center and harassing him— deserves serious consideration. How far should white "see"?: **1. ... Qxa6 2. Qxc5**.

This is the first *support position*—a snapshot we can use in our analysis as a starting point for diverging lines. Black has two reasonable replies: 2. ... Qe6 and 2. ... Nd7. Let's take on the easiest task first: 2. ... Nd7 3. Bc6 f6 (to guard e5) 4. Qd6, double-attacking the knight and rook, winning.

That leaves 2. ... Qe6, and now 3. Bc6+ Nd7 (not 3. ... Kd8 4. Bd2 b4 5. Qa5+) 4. Bxd7+

Kxd7 5. Qa7+

A brief look at this position should confirm that white has at least equal chances, and thus should play 1. Ra6!.

The actual game continued 5. ... Kc6 (not 5. ... Kc8 6. Bd2, but 5. ... Kd6 merited some analysis: 6. f4 f6 7. fxe5+ fxe5 8. Bf4 exf4 9. Qxd4+, and while white might not be winning, he certainly shouldn't lose) 6. Bd2 Rhc8 7. e4 Qb3 8. Ra1

8. ... b4 (8. ... Rb6 9. Rc1+) 9. Ra6+ Kb5 10. Ra5+ Kc6 11. Qc5+ Kd7 12. Ra7+ 1:0

In the two games above, two world champions, Garry Kasparov and Alexander Alekhine, made sacrifices that resulted in their winning. Both sacrificed an Exchange, but the first game showed a *positional* sacrifice, while the second demonstrated a *tactical* sacrifice.

Level III, Lesson Twenty-Two
Memory Markers!

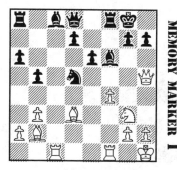

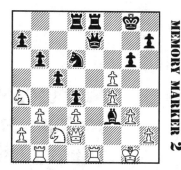

After 1. Qe2-h5

After 1. Rd1-e1

MEMORY MARKER 1

MEMORY MARKER 2

Black to move

White to move

MEMORY MARKER 3

MEMORY MARKER 4

Solutions:

MM1: 1. ... g6! 2. Bxg6 Qe7!!. Black returns a pawn, and emerges on top, after 3. Bxf6 Nxf6 4. Qf3 Rb8 5. Bd3 Bb7. (Olafson—Tal, 1959)

MM2: 1. ... Qe2 2. Rxe2 Rxe2, and here Smyslov plays 3. Qxe2, rather than expose himself to a deadly attack after 3. Qc1 Rg2+. (Smyslov—Tal, 1959)

MM3: 1. ... Rxd3 (preventing the looming attack) **2. Rxd3 Be4 3. Rd2 Qxc4 4. Rfd1 Bd5** (to stop 5. Rd8) **5. h3** (a trap—if 5. ... Qxa2, 6. Rxd5) **5. ... f5!**, and black is fine. (Maroczy—Rubinstein, 1907)

MM4: 1. Nd5!. An archetypal sacrifice. After 1. ... exd5 2. exd5 f5 3. Rde1, it's certainly more fun for white! (Tal—Larsen, 1965)

"Every cramped position
contains the germs of
defeat," diagnosed
Doctor Siegbert Tarrasch,
one of the strongest players
of the 19th century and
a practicing M.D.
The side with the isolani is
anything but cramped!

Lesson Twenty-Three
The Isolani

*The queen-pawn-isolani can be a
strength or a weakness. In this lesson, you
learn the techniques required to play with or against it.*

You've already learned what an isolated pawn is. It can be any pawn on the board. But a lot of modern strategy revolves around openings that produce an isolated queen pawn.

When we speak about positions with an isolated pawn (*isolani*), we usually mean the pawn structure that occurs, for example, after the following moves:

**1. e4 c6 2. d4 d5 3. exd5 cxd5
4. c4 Nf6 5. Nc3 e6 6. Nf3 Be7
7. cxd5 Nxd5 8. Bd3 0-0 9. 0-0**

The same pawn structure, and the same (or very similar) position can and does occur from many openings: The Caro-Kann (above), Nimzo-Indian, Queen's

"He who is afraid of the isolani should not play chess."

—Dr. Siegbert Tarrasch

Gambit Accepted, Queen's Gambit Orthodox, Sicilian Defense (Smith-Morra, Alapin), Alekhine Defense.

Black also often acquires an isolani:

1. d4 d5 2. c4 e6 3. Nc3 c5 (Tarrasch Defense) 4. cxd5 exd5 5. Nf3 Nf6 6. g3 (Rubinstein Variation) 6. ... Nc6 7. Bg2 cxd4 8. Nxd4

The main (often only) distinction in white's or black's ownership of the isolani is a single tempo—sufficient to determine who struggles for equality and who may aim higher.

There is also another, much more rarely occurring, type of *isolani*, where the queen-four-pawn is opposed not by the e-pawn but by the c-pawn.

After **1. e4 e6 2. d4 d5 3. Nd2 c5
4. exd5 exd5 5. dxc5 Bxc5**
Yes, an isolated pawn might

occur on another file, or another rank—but very rarely in any major openings, and such a pawn usually is by itself an obvious weakness. (Of course, such a weakness might be fully compensated by other factors, as is the case with backward pawns and any other pawn weaknesses).

With "our" isolated pawn (d4/d5), however, positions are *almost* balanced, very frequently occurring, full of life—and thus deserving of in-depth study.

Advantages and disadvantages of the isolani on d4

Plusses

• Space ("every cramped position contains the germs of defeat"—Dr. Tarrasch) and therefore ...

• Control of the semi-open e-file, including ...

• The e5-square (a likely place for the f3-knight to go), and often

• Pressure along the c-file

Minuses

• The isolani can't be defended by another pawn and thus requires protection by pieces.

• The d5-square in front of the isolani is a very good square for black's b7-bishop to control (a long diagonal) and for his pieces (a knight; later in the game, a queen or a rook) to occupy.

Main Plans

For white:

• If ahead in development, which is often the case — push d4-d5. White will be better after this opening of the position. (Unfortunately this isn't often possible.)

• Attack (positions often allow it, sometimes even demand it).

• More rarely: play over the c-file.

For black:

• Watch out for d4-d5 breaks (not all should be avoided).

• Simplify to diffuse the coming attack.

• Remember, endings are usually good for you.

The owner of the isolani has his chances in the middlegame, as the isolated pawn often becomes a weakness in the endgame.

Botvinnik—Vidmar
Nottingham, 1936

After 16. ... Nbxd5

17. f4!

White is planning to play f4-f5, in order to create a new file for his attack, and also extends the diagonal for his bishop on b3. Thanks to Botvinnik, this plan is now the standard in such positions.

17. ... Rc8 18. f5 exf5 19. Rxf5 Qd6

20. Nxf7!

The logical follow-up to white's plan. The rest is simple: 20. ... Rxf7 21. Bxf6 Bxf6 22. Rxd5 Qc6 23. Rd6 Qe8 24. Rd7, black resigned.

♚♚♚♚♚

In the following example, black found a way to force a very favorable ending.

Regedzinsky—Rubinstein
Lodz, 1917

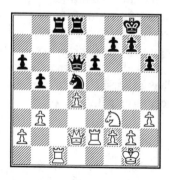

1. ... Qf4! 2. Rc2 (not 2. Qxf4 Nxf4 3. Rec2 Ne2+) **2. ... Qxd2 3. Rexd2 Rxc2 4. Rxc2 Nb4**

White faces a Hobson's choice, to give up a pawn with 5. Rc7, or to play 5. Rb2 (or Re2), abandoning the c-file to black (5. ... Rc8, with good winning chances).

Of course, not all endgames are so bad for the side with an isolani; many are, even if somewhat worse, easily defensible.

Transformations

Isolani positions can, of course, transition into other pawn structures. The following game begins with black's isolani, but white's d4-knight then captures black's knight on c6, and black recaptures with ... bxc6.

Petrosian—Spassky
World Championship match
2nd game, 1969

After 17. Qd3

So white transforms black's isolani into a d5/c6 pair. White plans to pressure the c-pawn on the semi-open file.

This position occurs in the Orthodox Defense of the Queen's Gambit Declined, Rubinstein Variation of the Tarrasch Defense, after the moves: 1. c4 e6 2. d4 d5 3. Nc3 c5 4. cxd5 exd5 5. Nf3 Nc6 6. g3 Nf6 7. Bg2 Be7 8. 0–0 0–0 9. Bg5 cxd4 10. Nxd4 h6 11. Be3 Bg4 12. Nb3 Be6 13. Rc1 Re8 14. Nb5 Qd7 15. N5d4 Bh3 16. Nxc6 bxc6 17. Qd3

Despite the change in pawn structure, many rules governing an isolani remain valid, as we can see from black's **17. ... Bxg2!**

Why not a tempo-grabbing 17. ... Bf5?—after all, the g2-bishop no longer targets the d5-pawn (protected now by its neighbor). The answer: exchange of the g2-bishop weakens the white king's position. Black may be able to launch a successful attack.

18. Kxg2 a5 19. Rc2

If 19. Nc5, then 19. ... Bxc5 20. Bxc5 Ne4, with an attack in mind; if 19. Bc5, then 19. ... Bd8, keeping more pieces on board.

19. ... a4

20. Nd2 (Safer was 20. Nc5, with equality.) **20. ... Qb7 21. Kg1 Rac8 22. Rfc1 Nd7 23. Nf3 c5**

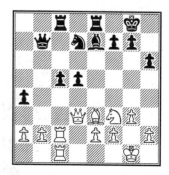

Another transformation: black acquires *hanging pawns* on c5 and d5. The position remained close to equal—and very complex. Indeed, the game was drawn after 61 moves.

Level III, Lesson Twenty-Three
Memory Markers!

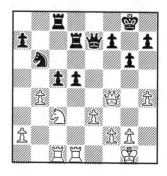

After 1. (b2)-b4

MEMORY MARKER 1

Solution:

MM1: 1. ... c4!, with a small advantage for white. Allowing the isolani on d5 is even worse, while the active 1. ... d4 (or 1. ... cxb4 2. Nxd5) loses material to 2. Ne4 Nd5 3. Qf3.

**Every chess player
should have
his own
opening secrets.**

Lesson Twenty-Four

Choose Your (Opening) Weapons!

*As you approach Expert level, you'll need a
repertoire of openings you have confidence in.
This lesson will provide some advice.*

In previous centuries, before a duel, the challenged party got to "choose his weapons." In chess, both parties have a say into what the opening turns out to be, which may not be clear for a number of moves. But the idea of being more adept with certain opening "weapons," and trying to see that your favorite variations are played, is certainly a valid idea.

On an advanced level, opening study requires more resources than any single book on chess can provide. The idea of owning a repertoire—openings that you know and trust that cover whatever your opponent might play—is, frankly, a basic survival skill in tournament chess at the expert and master level.

Our general advice is to keep playing the openings you've been playing (as long as they are some of the many master-approved beginnings, which means almost any opening that has a name), rather than changing to new openings. "Opening-shopping" can become a bad habit that both limits your experience with your opening repertoire and takes too much time away from studying the middlegame and ending. Instead of switching openings, try to find improvements within the openings you already know. (Remember, don't spend more than 25% of whatever study time you have for chess on openings.)

On the other hand, there are legitimate reasons to consider

changing:

a) If, after certain openings, the positions you reach are consistently poor;

b) If, even though you get decent positions in a few games after the opening stage, you find that the resulting positions aren't to your taste, or don't fit your abilities (for example, if you have a normal memory and little time to study openings, then razor-sharp, long lines of the Meran Variation aren't right for you)—it may be time for a change!

Try systematically to improve your knowledge and command of the openings you play. After each game, take a moment to check your opening moves against "theory," i.e., an opening book, whether it's a monograph—a whole book on a single opening—or all-inclusive books like the *Encyclopedia of Chess Openings* or *Modern Chess Openings*. Find what went right, or wrong, or in-between, who deviated first from the main line, and what "the book" says about that deviation. (If a move isn't mentioned—perhaps it's because that move was bad). The internet opens nearly limitless research possibilities on sites like www.chess.com and www.chess-games.com—but there are many others as well. Your main goal is to decide what you will play next

time if the same line occurs again in your game.

Some chess players manage to expand their opening repertoire in a scientific way. They examine their games, form an opinion about their style, strengths and weaknesses—and then look for the best-fitting openings. For instance, if you like endgames, consider, after 1. e4 e5 2. Nf3 Nc6 3. Bb5

Ruy Lopez
Black to move

3. ... a6 (black's main line) to continue 4. Bxc6 (the Exchange Variation) dxc6 5. d4 exd4 6.Qxd4

Most chess players, however, choose their new openings in a far-less-organized fashion, often by seeing an interesting, appealing position in a chess magazine, and saying "I'd like to be black in this position! Let's see how it happened!"

Some players even look for such discoveries in old books (and magazines). There is a Russian saying—"Everything new is well-forgotten old": some old lines were not refuted, but simply went out of fashion for no other reason than the constant flux (in some cases, rotation) of what is fashionable. This method of finding "new" ideas in old publications was often successfully used by Bobby Fischer, who borrowed, for instance, the following 19th-century (!) line from first world champion Wilhelm Steinitz:

1. e4 e5 2. Nf3 Nc6 3. Bc4 Nf6 (Two Knights' Defense) 4. Ng5 d5 5. exd5 Na5

6. Bb5+ c6 7. dxc6 bxc6 8. Be2 h6

By the 1960s, there was only one "theoretical" line in this position, 9. Nf3 e4 10. Ne5. But Fischer read that in the 1890s, the first world champion favored **9. Nh3!?**. Seventy years later, Bobby used this move to win one of his most famous games in the 1960s. The move then went out

of fashion again, only to be renewed 30 years later by world championship candidate Nigel Short. Today, it's considered equal to 9. Nf3. So the ideas of the "old" masters can not only surprise modern opponents—but can turn out to be just as good as the latest fashionable lines.

You may also try to create, or perhaps augment, your opening repertoire by choosing a "hero" and following his or her opening choices. ("Her" is not just a nod to political correctness—Judith and Susan Polgar, as well as several other female players, are great opening role-models.) Lev Alburt read, as a young master, Michael Botvinnik's superb book *100 Selected Games*. Soon after, Lev began, in Botvinnik's footsteps, playing Dutch Defense (1. ... f5 vs. 1. d4)—without, however, switching to the French, Botvinnik's most common choice in that book against 1. e4.

And your hero can be up–and-coming young American Hikaru Nakamura or German Siegbert Tarrasch, one of the strongest and most opinionated players of the late 19th century. Nakamura's opening choices are, objectively, somewhat better; Tarrasch's are simpler. (And Tarrasch's openings are still good enough to be successfully employed as high as the U.S. Championship!)

When attracted to a new opening, get a good book on it—preferably a book with more words than symbols, with titles like "Understanding Caro-Kann" or "Play the Smith-Morra." (Later, you may move to more advanced, "meatier" books.)

A *repertoire book* is a volume that puts together a whole system of playing either white or black, covering most reasonable moves your opponent may play in the opening. Such a book can also be very useful. In particular, we recommend *Chess Openings for Black, Explained, A Complete Repertoire*, and *Chess Openings for White, Explained, Winning with 1. e4!*, both by Lev Alburt, Roman Dzindzichashvili and Eugene Perelshteyn, with Al Lawrence. In the first book, we recommend, against 1. e4, the Hyper-Accelerated Dragon:

1. e4 c5 (the Sicilian) 2. Nf3 g6 3. d4 cxd4 4. Nxd4 Bg7 (the main line).

**Sicilian Defense
Hyper-Accelerated Dragon**

And here one of the two most popular moves is 5. c4, going into a variation known as the Maroczy Bind.

The openings within that book are interconnected, as they should be for a truly complete repertoire. Thus, against 1. c4, our book gives 1. ... c5, and after 2. Nf3—2. ... g6, which may lead to some of the same positions: 3. d4 cxd4 4. Nxd4 Bg7,

English Opening

and now 5. e4 transposes into the same Maroczy Bind position as in the Accelerated Dragon line above. Openings can flow into one another—this is called *transposing*. (Our choice against 1. d4 is a super-solid but lively Nimzo-Bogo complex: 1. ... Nf6 2. c4 e6 and now 3. Nc3 Bb4 is Nimzo, and 3. Nf3 Bb4+, the Bogo-Indian.)

The companion volume, *Chess Openings for White, Explained*, is subtitled "Winning with 1. e4," so our first move choice is clear. (Russian master and opening guru Vsevolod Rauser titled one of his articles "1.e4!, and White Is Winning." He—and we—don't, of course, mean "winning" literally, but rather getting winning chances. But "winning," or Fischer's famous recommendation, "1. e4!—best by test" sounds more encouraging, true?

And, as noted in chapter 19 of this book, each of our *Explained* volumes contains a section of about a hundred pages that reviews *all* remaining openings! You can read a little more about these two repertoire books at the back of this book.

If you don't have lots of time to study main-stream openings, look for shortcuts! (One type of shortcut is an old, forgotten line. In short, "Tarrasch's repertoire.") Just a few examples here (not necessarily Tarrasch's actual choices).

The Center-Counter:
1. e4 d5 2. exd5 Qxd5 3. Nc3

Center Counter

and now either 3. ... Qa5 (see chapter 19) or 3. ... Qd6. There's no reason that one can't make master, and even grandmaster, playing this defense, and it eliminates hundreds and hundreds of hours of study. And it's only one

example of a *shortcut*.

Against 1. d4, consider 1. ... e5 (Englund Gambit). And then 2. dxe5 Nc6 (3. ... d6 is another way to play: 4. exd6 Bxd6) 3. Nf3

Englund Gambit

(3. f4 f6 leads to unclear play) 3. ... Qe7 4. Qd5 (black must have something up his sleeve as well for 4. Bg5) 4. ... f6 5. exf6 Nxf6 6. Qb3 d5

Unlikely to succeed in a master section (although occasionally used by GMs against other GMs), this line may serve a Tal-inspired sacrificer well in Expert or lower groups.

With white, you can choose theory-free (well, almost) 1. b4—still leading, after all, to equality, or a "reverse" opening, such a 1. Nf3 d5 2. g3 c5 3. Bg2 Nc6 4. 0-0 e5 5. d3,

King's Indian Attack

the King's Indian Attack, where you, compared to the black side of the King's Indian Defense, have an extra tempo—enough to make your (white's) position *at least* equal.

Some final hints:

• Whenever possible, find your own opening moves, plans, schemes! (Recall "Be your own openings' Edison," from Chapter 19.)

• Study types of positions and pawn structures that are likely to occur in the openings you play. In some case, you can even study the kinds of *endgames* that result, for example from the Ruy Lopez, Exchange Variation at the beginning of this chapter.

Keep at it and your opening repertoire—although at first crude and incomplete, with many weak spots and gaps—will undoubtedly improve, expand and develop, mirroring your overall growth as a chess player.

Afterword:
Moving On to
Expert and Master

In this book, you've learned the fundamentals of good chess. In doing so, we believe that you've quite literally saved hundreds of hours compared to the normal process aspiring players go through, because of the unique curriculum we've presented. Still, to master chess, much like mastering a physical sport, you must continue playing.

• Playing in clubs—casually and seriously—is highly recommended.

• Playing in tournaments is also highly recommended.

• Playing serious, slower games with competitive players *somewhere* is a must.

• Playing blitz (fast games that give each player only five minutes or so to complete), including blitz games on the internet, is both fine training and a lot of fun.

Blitz chess develops qualities such as intuition, decisiveness, short-range (one to two moves deep) tactical vision, fundamental strategic knowledge (like capturing toward the center), a good feeling for time. Four-time U.S. Champion Yasser Seirawan says that he became a strong player by playing mainly blitz chess, but that's unusual!

On the other hand, a serious game (such as 90 minutes for the first 30 moves, followed by one hour per player for the rest of the game) develops the ability to calculate four to five moves deep, in-depth strategic thinking, and prophylactic habits. It also trains you to search for the best move. (Motto in blitz: "See a good move, make it." Motto for tournament chess: "See a good move—make a mental note of it, and search for a better one.")

Action chess—such as 30 minutes per game—falls somewhere between the two. All—in balance—are good for your chess growth!

Analyze your games, first by yourself, then with a computer, friend or coach. On average, spend at least one hour per each serious game! (Even if you play blitz, spend at least as much time examining a game—doing what chess players call a "post mortem"—as you spent playing it.

If you play fast chess on the

internet, at one of the serious sites like ChessClub.com, the score of your game, in the same algebraic notation used in this book, can be automatically saved to your computer and even be emailed to you. In addition, after your game, the good online sites will let you examine your game with the help of computer evaluation. That process can help immensely in finding where you or your opponent went wrong, and what combinations could have been played. (Computers are nearly unerring in finding or rejecting combinations.)

When playing a serious, slower game, besides keeping a score—which is your obligation in an official event—also record time spent on each move by you *and* by your opponent. Having a record you can analyze will help you evaluate your *time management*, an important element of the game. When doing a post mortem of a game, it's very useful to know how much time you spent on a certain move—too little (the most common mistake, especially in openings) or too much.

Some tips on making notes of time used:
• Don't record fractions of one minute.
• Stop recording the time when you feel yourself in time pressure—say you have 20 minutes

for six moves, but you're in a very sharp position. And don't worry (and don't blame yourself) if you missed writing down time for a move, or several moves—simply resume when you notice your lapse.

Take your time in the openings!

Take your time in making your opening moves, even if you "know the line." When you play the first moves, concentrate and envision what the game could look like after three or four more moves. Breathe before you move. Don't fall for the psychological trap of thinking you have to keep pace with an opponent who is banging the moves out. (It's a very old hustler's trick.) It's very, very disheartening to be saddled with a bad or even a lost game from the starting gate! So how long should you take for the beginning moves?

Rule-of-thumb time formula

As an example, let's assume you regularly play, as black, the Queen's Gambit Declined, Orthodox Defense. Tournament time controls of 90 minutes for 30 moves, or two hours for 40 require you to make, on average, a move every three minutes. On your first three moves, however, you'd spend no more than a minute: 1. d4 d5 2. c4 e6 3. Nc3 Nf6, so you've "banked" a full eight minutes.

(You haven't wasted time acting like you don't know what to play, but neither have you moved so quickly that you could have made a "finger mistake.") Here you expect 4. Bg5, to be met by baiting your favorite trap, 4. ... Nbd7.

But what if your opponent surprises you? A surprise can be mild, say 4. Nf3, when the game is likely to develop in a way familiar to you. A surprise can be pleasant, like 4. h3 or 4. Nb5 (wastes of time that can't be good), or threatening like 4. g4 (if you take, then 5. e4—then what?).

No matter how big or small a surprise is, here is the universal formula for managing your time: you should think on your next move *half the time saved so far, plus three "regular" minutes*— in our example, a total of seven minutes. This is, of course, a general guide. You may, and should, spend more on 4. Nb5 or g4 than on more "normal" moves like 4. Nf3.

Further Study

In Level One, you learned rules of chess—and how to apply those rules to win more games.

In the more expansive Level Two, you learned the fundamentals of the game: attack and defense, strategies and tactics, openings, middlegames and endings.

And in Level Three, you've begun to deal with truly advanced chessic matters, such as the queen fighting minor pieces, the bishop pair and the *isolani*.

Now that you've learned so much so quickly, it's time to learn to apply your knowledge effectively, through practice. It's also time to expand your understanding.

To make sure you're solid in your knowledge of fundamentals, browse through the *Comprehensive Chess Course*, volume two, by Pelts and Alburt. Then go to our books on Tactics (volume 3), Attack and Defense (volume 4), Strategy (volume 5), and Endings (volume 7). You'll find these, and other books making the extended *Comprehensive Chess Course: from beginner to master and beyond*, on the last page of this book.

We'd recommend that you complement our course by simultaneously reading other, relevant works. For instance, while reading our *Just the Facts (Winning Endgame Knowledge)*, glance into the relevant parts of Pandolfini's *Endgame Course* (relatively light reading) and Dvoretsky's *Endgame Manual* (anything but light).

Most of all, enjoy yourself while mastering chess! You'll meet no end of fascinating people and never tire of unwrapping the wonderful mysteries of the world's greatest strategy game!

Glossary and Index of Key Terms

(Italicized numbers in parentheses refer to pages.)

Algebraic notation: Method of recording moves in which each square is named, also using special symbols *(26-27)*.

Back-rank mate: A checkmate delivered by a queen or rook against a king blocked in on his first rank *(16, 82)*.

Backward pawn: A pawn whose neighboring pawns have been pushed forward. Backward pawns may be weak due to lack of protection by other pawns *(160)*.

Bad bishop: A bishop blocked by pawns *(111-114)*.

Battery: Any two friendly, long-range pieces lined up along one line of attack *(68)*.

Bishop: A minor piece that moves diagonally *(18)*.

Bishop Fortress: A drawing formation available in some BOC endings *(227-228)*.

Bishop pair: The possession of two bishops versus bishop and knight, or two knights *(261-267)*.

Bishops of opposite color: (Abbreviated "BOC.") When each opponent has one bishop, one controlling the light squares and the other controlling dark *(114)*.

Breakthrough: Creating a far-advanced passed pawn with a sacrifice *(p. 73)*.

Castling: A move bringing your king into safety and your rook into play *(21)*.

Center: The squares e4, d4, e5, and d5; the prime real estate of the board *(45)*.

Check: A move attacking the king *(15)*.

Checkmate: The goal of chess, when the losing king is in check and can't escape *(16)*.

Chessboard: Our battlefield *(11)*.

Chess clock: Two timers connected to keep track of each individual's time during a game.

Clearance: Vacating a critical square to open a line or square *(85)*.

Combination: A series of forced moves to gain some advantage *(70)*.

Decoy: The tactic of forcing your opponent to go to an unfavorable square *(81)*.

Deflection: Coaxing a piece or pawn away from its post *(81)*.

Desperado: A kamikaze piece *(87)*.

Development: Moving the pieces from their starting squares to better squares in the opening *(44-45)*.

Diagonal: A slanted row of squares of the same color *(11)*.

Discovered attack: A surprise attack created when one chessman moves to uncover an attack by another *(79)*.

Discovered check: A type of discovered attack that places the king in check *(80)*.

Double attack: A tactic which threatens two or more enemy men simultaneously *(36)*.

Double check: A discovered check that puts the king in check from two different directions. The only way out is to move the king *(80)*.

Doubled pawns: Two friendly pawns occupying the same file, often but not always weak *(158)*.

Doubled rooks: Two friendly rooks occupying the same rank or file, forming a battery *(106, 132, 137)*.

Draw: A tie game, which can happen one of six different ways *(42-44)*.

Draw by perpetual check: A draw resulting from unending checks *(44)*.

Draw by repetition: A draw resulting from repeating a position three times, not necessarily consecutively *(43)*.

Endgame: The third and final stage of the game, in which few pieces remain *(44-45, 165-235)*; easiest and least winnable *(185)*; reasons to study *(164)*.

En passant: "In passing," a special pawn capture *(22)*.

En prise: The state of being attacked and undefended.

Exchange v. exhange: With an upper-case "E," winning a rook for a bishop or a knight; lower-case "e," a trade *(34)*.

FIDE: Also "World Chess Federation," the governing "United Nations" of chess; website: www.fide.com.

Fianchetto: Development of the bishop to b2, g2, b7, or g7 *(152)*.

Fifty-move rule: A draw after 50 moves without any capture or pawn move *(43)*.

File: A vertical row of squares running between the two opponents *(11-12)*.

Forfeit: The loss of a game due to overstepping the time limit or a penalty imposed by the tournament director.

Fork: See "Double attack."

Gambit: A material sacrifice in the opening (usually a pawn) in exchange for initiative *(280)*.

Good biship: An unblocked bishop with good mobility *(111-112, 130)*.

Improving your position: Important concept in winning chess *(40)*.

Intiative: The ability to make threats.

Interference: A tactic used to disrupt the interaction of your opponent's forces *(83)*.

Isolani: Isolated d-pawn that occurs in some modern openings, providing a strategic argument *(287-291)*.

King: The most valuable piece in a chess game *(14)*.

King safety: Prime directive: keep your king safe behind a wall of pawns until the danger of checkmate is reduced.

Kingside: The half of the board from the e-file to the h-file, where the kings originate.

King's Fortress: A drawing formation available in some BOC endings *(227-229)*.

Knight: The only chess piece that jumps *(19)*.

Lucena's position: Illustrates a technique to win certain common rook endgames *(205)*.

Major pieces: The rooks and queen *(13, 17)*.

Material advantage: Having a higher "value-count" than the opposing army *(33, 34)*.

Middlegame: The second of three phases of a game *(44)*.

Minor pieces: The bishops and knights *(18-19)*.

Opening: The first of three phases of a chess game, when the players develop their pieces *(44, 243-259, 293-298)*.

Opposition: A technique used by a king to gain key squares *(170-174)*.

Outpost: A well-placed piece in enemy territory; see also "strong square" *(129-136)*.

Outside passed pawn: A passed pawn distant from other pawns, a powerful asset in an endgame *(178)*.

Overloading: When a piece has too many duties *(84)*.

Overprotection: The protection of a key piece, pawn or square by more pieces and pawns than are immediately necessary.

Pawns: The foot soldiers of chess are not called pieces *(20)*; — *chain*: diagonally adjacent pawns of the same color *(41, 114, 263)*; *evaluating* — *(156)*; *isolated* —: a pawn with no friendly pawns on the files adjacent to it *(158, 220, 287-291)*; — *island*: adjacent, friendly pawns *(p. 156)*; *passed* —: a pawn with no opposing pawns on adjacent files *(155)*; *poisoned* —: a pawn as bait that should not be taken *(35)*; — *promotion*: a pawn reaching the opposing back-rank must become a piece (but not a king) of its master's choice *(22)*; — *structure*: the configuration of the pawns *(157)*; — *storm*: an attack on the enemy position by several pawns *(103)*; — *weaknesses (157)*.

Philidor's position: Illustrates a drawing method available in some rook vs. rook-and-pawn endings *(203)*.

Pieces: Kings, queens, rooks, bishops, and knights are the *pieces* in chess, as opposed to pawns.

Pin: A tactic that "pins down" one piece to another, usually more valuable one *(79)*.

Positional: Concerned with a game's strategic, long-term effects, as opposed to tactics.

Queen: The most powerful piece *(16)*.

Queenside: The half of the chessboard from the d-file to the a-file.

Rank: A horizontal row that runs across the board, numbered 1 through 8 *(11-12)*.

Rook: The second most powerful piece *(13)*.

Rook lift: Moving a rook off the back rank *(95)*.

Rule of the square: A helpful analytical tool to determine quickly whether a lone king can catch an enemy passed pawn *(177-178)*.

Sacrifice: Giving up material to gain some other advantage *(91-96; 279-285)*.

Semi-open game: A game that starts 1. e4, answered with a move other than 1. ... e5.

Skewer: The shish kebab of tactics *(37)*.

Smothered mate: An embarrassing mate delivered by a knight to a king blocked by his own army *(72)*.

Stalemate: A position in which there are no legal moves for the player on move, and the player's king is not in check, making the game a draw *(23)*.

Strategy: Dealing with overall plans, as opposed to tactical calculations *(108-109)*.

Strong square: An important square available to your piece, usually inside enemy territory; see also "Outpost" *(151-155)*.

Tactics: The fireworks of chess. These are tricks or weapons used to win material or gain some other advantage *(77-88)*.

Time control: A designated time allowance for a certain number of moves.

Touch move: If you touch a piece without first saying "I adjust" or "j'adoube," you must move it to any legal square.

Trading: See "Exchange v. exchange."

Triangulation: An endgame technique in which the king takes two moves to get to a square he could have gone to in one move, thus intentially "losing a move" *(187)*.

Under-promotion: Promoting a pawn to a rook, bishop, or knight rather than a queen; very rare.

United States Chess Federation: Also "USCF," the official governing body of chess in the U.S., with a wealth of free information at www.uschess.org.

Value of the chessmen: Points, from 1 (pawn) to 9 (queen), assigned as a general guide to the value of the men; see also "Material Advantage" *(24)*.

Visualization: Imagining the board and pieces in your mind; a crucial skill exercise *(30)*.

Weak square: Broadly speaking, your opponent's "Strong square," see above *(151-155)*.

Windmill attack: A combination in which a piece captures several enemy pieces by means of repeated discovered attacks, usually on the king, *(64)*

Winning the Exchange: See "Exchange v. exchange."

Zugzwang: A situation in which any move will make the position worse *(p. 72)*.

It's Easy to Order Books from Lev Alburt!

Yes! I want to improve fast—to Master & beyond!

Comprehensive Chess Course:

- ☐ Vol. 1 (126 pp.) $16.95
- ☐ Vol. 2 (304 pp.) $28.95
- ☐ Vol. 3 (246 pp.) $19.95
- ☐ Vol. 4 (256 pp.) $19.95
- ☐ Vol. 5 (356 pp.) $24.95
- ☐ Vol. 6 (188 pp.) $17.95
- ☐ Vol. 7 (412 pp.) $26.95
- ☐ Vol. 8 (208 pp.) $18.95

- ☐ *Pirc Alert! (448 pp.) $34.95*
- ☐ *Chess Rules of Thumb (192 pp.) $19.95*
- ☐ *Three Days with Bobby Fischer and other chess essays (288 pp.) $29.95*
- ☐ *Chess Openings for White, Explained (548 pp.) $29.95*
- ☐ *Chess Openings for Black, Explained (552 pp.) $29.95*

- ☐ *Building Up Your Chess (352 pp.) $29.95*
- ☐ *Chess for the Gifted and Busy (304 pp.) $19.95*

Send the volumes I've checked above to:

Name_____

Street Address or PO Box _____

City_____State_____Zip Code_____

(optional) Here's the inscription I'd like above GM Lev Alburt's autograph!

_____

Books autographed free if you send check or money order to:

GM Lev Alburt, PO Box 534, Gracie Station, NY, NY 10028

(Add $4.95 for shipping for any number of books! NY residents add sales tax.)

For credit card orders call: 800-247-6553

(Sorry, autographs are not available on credit card orders.)

For more about chess and chess books—
and for information on personal lessons
from Grandmaster Lev Alburt, go to:

www.chesswithlev.com

or call

212.794.8706

3 1170 00880 3243